CITYPACK TOP 25
Las Vegas

JACKIE STADDON AND HILARY WESTON

AA Publishing
If you have any comments or suggestions for this guide you can contact the editor at
Citypack@theAA.com

How to Use This Book

This guide is divided into four sections
• Essential Las Vegas: An introduction to the city and tips on making the most of your stay.
• Las Vegas by Area: We've broken the city into five areas, and recommended the best sights, shops, entertainment venues, nightlife and restaurants in each one. Suggested walks help you to explore on foot.
• Where to Stay: The best hotels, whether you're looking for luxury, budget or something in between.
• Need to Know: The info you need to make your trip run smoothly, including getting about by public transportation, weather tips, emergency phone numbers and useful websites.

Navigation In the Las Vegas by Area chapter, we've given each area its own color, which is also used on the locator maps throughout the book and the map on the inside front cover.

Maps The fold-out map accompanying this book is a comprehensive street plan of Las Vegas. The grid on this fold-out map is the same as the grid on the locator maps within the book. We've given grid references within the book for each sight and listing.

Contents

CONTENTS

Introducing Las Vegas

Las Vegas is the entertainment capital of the world, where sleep is a mere inconvenience interrupting a continuous stream of fun and hedonism, and where everything is bigger, louder, flashier and trashier than anywhere else in the world.

From the moment you cruise into town it will strike you that this is like no other place. The sheer scale of everything is overwhelming, and the Strip (Las Vegas Boulevard South) in all its blazing glory is a thing of wonderment. Where else can you capture a skyscape that includes the Eiffel Tower, St. Mark's Campanile, an Egyptian pyramid and the Statue of Liberty on the same block?

Evolving from the early saloons, the first casinos and hotels were built in the Downtown area in the 1930s, followed by the expansion of the Strip in the 1940s. So what continues to bring millions of visitors here annually—gambling millions of dollars in the process? Las Vegas is an ever-evolving metropolis with a restless spirit that is part of its electric appeal. Hotels are regularly being torn down to make way for brand-new innovative ideas, and entertainment programs constantly change. Vegas now boasts some of the top restaurants in the world, many run by celebrity chefs, and most top designer names have made their mark on the shopping scene.

You might be forgiven for believing Las Vegas is not synonymous with culture. But beyond the neon there are some great museums and galleries, and ballet and opera blend perfectly with light entertainment. A few miles away from the man-made wonders are dramatic canyons, dams, and sparkling lakes, and the terrain lends itself to some of the finest golf courses. No matter how you spend your time here, this crazy city will never let you forget that the driving force is gambling. And there is one thing you can gamble on—Vegas once seen is never forgotten.

Facts + Figures

- There are more than 15,000 miles (24,000km) of neon tubing in the Strip and Downtown Las Vegas.
- There are on average 315 weddings per day in Vegas.
- There are more than 200,000 slot machines to take your cash.

RAT PACK MEETS VEGAS

In the 1960s, Las Vegas was dominated by a group of stars collectively known as the Rat Pack. Frank Sinatra first performed at the Sands Hotel in 1960, with John F. Kennedy in the audience. Thereafter, Sinatra, along with Dean Martin, Sammy Davis Jr., Peter Lawford and Joey Bishop—collectively the Rat Pack—dominated the scene and drew the crowds in droves.

TYING THE KNOT IN STYLE

Thousands of people are following in the footsteps of the rich and famous and saying "I do" in Vegas. Famous couples such as Elvis and Priscilla Presley have been joined by Mr and Mrs Average from countries as far apart as Britain and Japan, to get married in some of the 50 or so wedding chapels (▷ 76).

HOW IT BEGAN

Spawned from a trading post along the old Spanish Trail, Las Vegas became a popular stop for its freshwater spring. The prospect of gold added to the lure and later the building of the Hoover Dam secured the city's future. The liberal state laws of Nevada allowed the growth of the casinos, and soon the little campsite in the fearsome heat and inhospitable desert developed into a city.

A Short Stay
in Las Vegas

DAY 1

Morning Start the day with a leisurely breakfast at the **Rainforest Café** (▷ panel, 42) in the MGM Grand. From here you can be ready and waiting in line at 11am for the opening of the **Lion Habitat** (▷ 26–27) right next door, where you can see the big cats in action.

Mid-morning Cross the walkway to **New York-New York** (▷ 31) to take an exhilarating ride on the roller coaster. Head up the Strip to the **Bellagio** (▷ 46) and enjoy the spectacular dancing fountain show before going inside for a spot of culture at the **Bellagio Gallery of Fine Art** (▷ 59).

Lunch Move on to **Caesars Palace** (▷ 47) for lunch at one of the hotel's many superb eating options.

Afternoon Pass through the hotel, trying not to be tempted by the slot machines, to the Forum shops. Partake in some upscale retail therapy under ever-changing skies, and be sure to see the talking statues that come alive throughout the day. Return to the street and take the moving walkway into the **Mirage** (▷ 52–53). The highlight here is the **Dolphin Habitat and the Secret Garden** (▷ 48–49) to the rear of the hotel.

Dinner Proceed to Treasure Island and take the walkway across the Strip to the **Venetian** (▷ 56–57). After a short wander, take an early dinner and soak up the romantic atmosphere in St. Mark's Square.

Evening After dinner, go back over the walkway to try to catch the 7pm showing of the **Sirens of TI** (▷ 61). If the huge crowds deter you, see the volcano erupt into the night sky at the Mirage, then go to a late performance of your favorite show (reserve in advance). After the show, try your luck at the tables until the early hours.

Morning Relax over breakfast at Raffles Café in the **Mandalay Bay** (▷ 112), which has a veranda overlooking the pool area. After you've eaten, visit the hotel's main attraction, **Shark Reef** (▷ 32–33).

Mid-morning Hop on the monorail to the **Excalibur** (▷ 24–25), stopping at **Luxor** (▷ 28–29) to visit the Titanic Exhibition. Excalibur has some great family entertainment and a fun atmosphere.

Lunch Don't leave the Excalibur without sampling the RoundTable buffet. With your appetite satisfied, cross the walkway to the Tropicana.

Afternoon You should arrive here just in time to see the 2pm showing of **Dirk Arthur's Xtreme Magic** show (▷ 34; not on Friday). Leave the Tropicana and walk past MGM Grand to the **Miracle Mile** (▷ 55) shopping mall—pop in to pick up a few things if you feel the need. Otherwise continue to **Paris Las Vegas** (▷ 54), and take the elevator up the Eiffel Tower for one of the best views of the city. Catch the monorail from here to the **Venetian** (▷ 56–57), where you can visit **Madame Tussaud's** (▷ 51). To finish the afternoon, treat yourself to a ride on a gondola down the canal.

Dinner Catch the Deuce bus downtown to the Queens hotel for a real dining experience at **Hugo's Cellar** (▷ 93); reservations are recommended.

Evening Walk back to Fremont Street to be mesmerized by the **Fremont Street Experience** (▷ 88). After you've seen the show, wander a while and enjoy the party atmosphere, before taking a taxi back to the Strip to join the night owls at a club; try **Studio 54** (▷ 40) or **Tryst** (▷ 81).

Bellagio ▷ 46 Tuscan-theme resort that takes you to the lovely Italian town on Lake Como.

Caesars Palace and the Forum ▷ 47 Fountains and Corinthian columns celebrate the glory of Rome.

Circus Circus ▷ 72–73 Step inside the big top to find aerialists, acrobats, jugglers and clowns.

Dolphin Habitat and the Secret Garden ▷ 48–49 A secure haven for amazing big cats and lovable dolphins.

Downtown ▷ 86–87 If you're looking for classic Las Vegas, this is the place to find it.

Excalibur ▷ 24–25 Cross the drawbridge into this fantasyland to join King Arthur and his knights.

Fremont Street Experience ▷ 88 Be dazzled by this amazing light-and-sound show.

Hoover Dam and Lake Mead ▷ 98–99 A must-see getaway from the neons.

Imperial Palace Auto Collections ▷ 50 The world's largest and finest classic car showroom.

Las Vegas Natural History Museum ▷ 89 An animated dinosaur exhibit takes center stage here.

Liberace Museum ▷ 30 The ultimate shrine to glitz and glamor, and the showman who epitomizes them.

Lion Habitat ▷ 26–27 A lion habitat enclosed by a glass wall for a unique encounter with big cats.

Luxor ▷ 28–29 Egypt, the *Titanic* and the human body–a strange combination, but true.

Madame Tussaud's ▷ 51 Wax figures of the world's famous come to life in amusing circumstances.

The Mirage ▷ 52–53 White tigers, dolphins and other exotic animals in a tropical atmosphere.

NASCAR Café and Speed: The Ride ▷ 74 Race car fans and adrenalin junkies will love it.

New York-New York ▷ 31 The best of the Big Apple all one-third scale, and a sky-high roller coaster.

Paris Las Vegas ▷ 54 Paris captured with replicas of the Eiffel Tower and Arc de Triomphe.

Planet Hollywood and Miracle Mile ▷ 55 Glamorous film premieres and red carpet events.

Red Rock Canyon ▷ 100–101 Spectacular rock formations a 20-minute drive from Vegas.

Shark Reef ▷ 32–33 This exciting undersea world represents more than 100 different species.

Stratosphere Tower ▷ 75 White-knuckle rides at the top of the tallest free-standing tower in the US.

The Venetian ▷ 56–57 Winding canals and authentic gondolas help re-create the romantic Italian city.

Wedding Chapels ▷ 76 Getting married in a Las Vegas wedding chapel is an event you will never forget.

Wynn Las Vegas ▷ 77 Class and sophistication ooze from this sparkling bronze tower.

These pages are a quick guide to the Top 25, which are described in more detail later. Here they are listed alphabetically and the tinted background shows which area they are in.

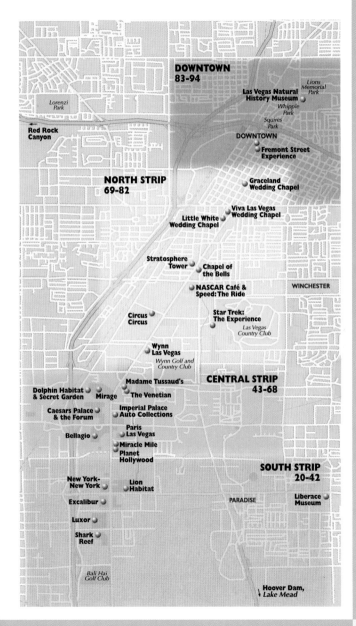

DOWNTOWN
83–94

Lions Memorial Park

Las Vegas Natural History Museum

Whipple Park

Squires Park

Lorenzi Park

Red Rock Canyon

DOWNTOWN

Fremont Street Experience

NORTH STRIP
69–82

Graceland Wedding Chapel

Viva Las Vegas Wedding Chapel

Little White Wedding Chapel

Stratosphere Tower

Chapel of the Bells

WINCHESTER

NASCAR Café & Speed: The Ride

Circus Circus

Star Trek: The Experience

Las Vegas Country Club

Wynn Las Vegas

Wynn Golf and Country Club

CENTRAL STRIP
43–68

Madame Tussaud's

Dolphin Habitat & Secret Garden

Mirage

The Venetian

Caesars Palace & the Forum

Imperial Palace Auto Collections

Paris Las Vegas

Bellagio

Miracle Mile

Planet Hollywood

New York-New York

Lion Habitat

SOUTH STRIP
20–42

PARADISE

Liberace Museum

Excalibur

Luxor

Shark Reef

Bali Hai Golf Club

Hoover Dam, Lake Mead

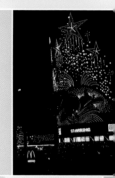

Shopping

Retail therapy in Vegas has soared in recent years, with an influx of designer stores and hundreds of well-known retailers and flagship department stores that have put the city firmly on the shopping map. Shopping in Vegas mainly revolves around treading the elegant walkways of the numerous malls. As for choice, it depends more on how much money you have to spend and how far you are prepared to travel than on what you are looking to buy.

A Unique Experience

Most of the Strip hotels have their own shopping opportunities, some more spectacular than others. There is simply no other city in the world where you are able to shop under an artificial sky among Roman architecture and talking statues or journey between shops by gondola, all within a short distance of each other. Hotel malls in Vegas offer more than just great stores: all sorts of entertainment is lined up to amuse you as you shop, but this is reflected in the cost of the goods. There are other malls on the Strip not attached to any particular hotel, such as the huge Fashion Show Mall (▷ 79), where you can browse through the boutiques while a fashion show takes place alongside.

Let's Get Serious

Serious shoppers should venture a few blocks away from the Strip, where they will discover more vast malls that are less crowded and filled

Wynn Esplanade (above middle) is one of many chic hotel malls to explore in Las Vegas

---

PAWNSHOPS

The nature of Vegas means it attracts lots of pawnshops. Many are opposite gambling areas—open 24 hours—ready and waiting to unload desperate gamblers of their possessions for quick cash. Items that are not reclaimed within about 120 days are sold. You will discover all sorts of bizarre items at pawnshops, but jewelry, musical instruments and electrical equipment are the most common. Gone are the days of acquiring these items at rock-bottom prices, although you might pick up the odd bargain.

with major retailers and specialist stores selling practical items at more realistic prices. Clothes range from daring and trendy to boutique exclusives, and the very latest in shoes, lingerie, jewelry and designer glasses complete a look suitable to hit the Vegas scene. True bargain-hunters should head for one of the factory outlets (▷ 92), where top designer clothes, among other things, can be bought at 25–75 percent off. Items for the home, electronics and footwear are particularly good value. A lot of the merchandise is end of line or last season's items. Just make sure you are getting top quality and not seconds or damaged goods. Some outlet malls have a shuttle service from hotels on the Strip.

Souvenirs and Gifts

At the other end of the scale from the classy boutiques are the endless souvenir shops along Las Vegas Boulevard, each selling the same mass-produced card decks and key rings. Every hotel also has a gift shop, with logo merchandise that exploits themes to the extreme, while casino gift shops are generally more elegant and expensive. Whether you decide to shop on the Strip or in the malls farther afield, Las Vegas offers its own unique shopping experience that you will not find elsewhere.

THAT SPECIAL GIFT

Although Vegas is not known for one particular souvenir—apart from the kitsch in its gift shops—given the time and money, you can buy almost anything here. Gambling merchandise abounds in every guise and quality leather jackets bearing logos are popular. Wine makes a safe gift as Vegas has the largest public collection of fine wines in the world. You might discover that unique collectible you've always wanted—a signed Michael Jordan basketball or autographed Beatles poster. Precious jewels for sale in the city have included Ginger Rogers' engagement ring and the Moghul Emerald (the world's largest carved emerald), but these would break the bank—unless you strike it lucky of course.

There's fabulous retail therapy to be found at Fashion Show Mall (top right) and elsewhere

Shopping by Theme

Whether you're looking for a department store, a quirky boutique, or something in between, you'll find it all in Las Vegas. On this page shops are listed by theme. For a more detailed write-up, see the individual listings in Las Vegas by Area.

Las Vegas by Night

Vegas really comes alive after the sun goes down, and some of the best attractions are to be found during the twilight hour. Soak up a pulsating nightlife scene like no other—this is a great place to party.

Endless Variety

From casino lounges to clubs, pubs and cocktail bars, the possibilities for a fun night out are endless. Numerous nightspots provide the chance to dance until dawn. Ultra lounges are the latest trend, stylish spaces that attract a cutting-edge crowd, where DJs spin their vinyl but conversation takes priority. But this is Sin City, and there are several, not very well-concealed, strip joints scattered throughout. These can, however, be disregarded amid the sheer scale of everything else.

Only the Best

Las Vegas is infamous for its stage extravaganzas, which incorporate unbelievable special effects and have attracted some of the world's hottest superstars. Shows vary from Broadway musicals and spectacular productions to comedy and magic. Vegas also plays host to some of the world's biggest special events, such as world championship boxing matches. The top shows can be expensive and the most popular often need to be reserved well in advance. But the best show of all is free: walk the Strip after dark and be treated to the amazing performance of thousands of flashing neon lights.

Las Vegas is not called the entertainment capital of the world for nothing

GAMING

Where else could you continually be refueled with free drinks as you play the blackjack table or wait for the roulette wheel to stop spinning? But be careful not to lose it all in one night. If you're not a serious player, the slot machines are lots of fun, too. Strolling through the casinos people-watching is another great way to pass the time— weary gamblers desperately trying to claw back some of their losses, ecstatic cries of joy when their luck holds and the jangling of chips when the slots pay out.

Eating Out

Not formerly renowned for good cuisine, Las Vegas has certainly turned things around from the days of lining up for a buffet that focused on quantity rather than quality.

So What's on Offer?

For starters, the famous Vegas buffet has become much more exciting and provides something for everyone at a reasonable price. There are endless top-class establishments where you can feast on the superb culinary skills of Michelin-star chefs and there's also the opportunity to dine at a restaurant run by a famous chef. Ever since Wolfgang Puck started the trend here in the 1990s, plenty of new places have opened bearing the names of celebrity chefs. The sheer variety of cuisine that has emerged is astonishing, from Italian and Mexican to Mediterranean, Indian and Pacific Rim. Fast-food outlets still play an important role, as do traditional steak houses.

Dining Tips

It can be hard to get a table at high-end restaurants, especially on Friday and Saturday nights. Plan ahead—you can reserve up to 30 days in advance. Many of these open for dinner only. Mid-range eateries are more likely to be open all day, and you will not need a reservation for breakfast or lunch. Most major hotels have a fast-food court to grab a quick bite, and many have a buffet at breakfast, lunch and dinner. Buffet lines can be long, so allow plenty of time.

DINNER SHOWS

If your time is short in Las Vegas take advantage of one of the dinner shows on offer, where you can eat and be thoroughly entertained at the same time. Probably the most popular of these is Tournament of Kings at the Excalibur (▷ 25). Also making headlines is Tony n' Tina's Wedding (▷ 61) ⊠ Planet Hollywood Resort, 3367 Las Vegas Boulevard South ☎ 702/949-6450 for tickets ⏱ Mon–Sat 7pm, a wild-and-wacky show in which you are invited to join Tony and Tina for their wedding feast.

Restaurants have evolved into an attraction in themselves with a Las Vegas flavor

Restaurants by Cuisine

There are restaurants to suit all tastes and budgets in Las Vegas. On this page they are listed by cuisine. For a more detailed description of each restaurant, see Las Vegas by Area.

BUFFETS

Bay Side (▷ 41)
Bellagio Buffet (▷ 66)
Carnival World (▷ 66)
Garden Court (▷ 93)
Paradise Garden Buffet
(▷ 68)

CAFÉS AND PUBS

Binion's Coffee Shop
(▷ 93)
Il Fornaio Panetteria
(▷ 42)
Harley Davidson Café
(▷ 67)
Verandah High Tea (▷ 42)

FRENCH AND OTHER EUROPEAN

Bouchon (▷ 66)
Daniel Boulud Brasserie
(▷ 82)
Hugo's Cellar (▷ 93)
Joël Robuchon (▷ 42)
Mon Ami Gabi (▷ 68)
Picasso (▷ 68)
Red Square (▷ 42)
Top of the World (▷ 82)

INTERNATIONAL

Cathouse (▷ 41)
DJT (▷ 82)
Pampas Brazilian Grill
(▷ 68)

ITALIAN

Battista's Hole in the Wall
(▷ 66)
Canaletto (▷ 66)
Francesco's (▷ 67)
Valentino (▷ 68)

NORTH AMERICAN AND MEXICAN

Aureole (▷ 41)
Border Grill (▷ 41)
Bradley Ogden (▷ 66)
Doña Maria Tamales
(▷ 93)
Dos Caminos (▷ 66)
Emeril's (▷ 41)
House of Lords (▷ 67)
Postrio (▷ 68)
Toto's (▷ 42)

ORIENTAL/FUSION

China Grill (▷ 41)
Hyakumi (▷ 67)
Koi (▷ 67)
Kokomo's (▷ 67)
Lillie's Noodle House
(▷ 93)
Lotus of Siam (▷ 82)
Noodle Shop (▷ 42)
Ra (▷ 82)
Second Street Grill (▷ 93)

STEAKS AND SEAFOOD

Binion's Ranch Steakhouse
(▷ 93)
Charlie Palmer Steak (▷ 41)
Craftsteak (▷ 41)
Envy (▷ 82)
Kristofer's (▷ 82)
Lawry's The Prime Rib
(▷ 67)
Michael Mina (▷ 67)
Nero's (▷ 68)
Nobhill Tavern (▷ 42)
The Steakhouse (▷ 82)
Triple George Grill (▷ 93)
Village Seafood (▷ 68)

If You Like...

However you'd like to spend your time in Las Vegas, these top suggestions should help you tailor your ideal visit. Each sight or listing has a fuller write-up elsewhere in the book.

SOMETHING FOR FREE

You can't help but be drawn to the spectacular Bellagio Fountains (▷ 46).
Take a trip downtown to see the Fremont Street Experience (▷ 88), a dazzling display of images cast on an LED-light roof.
Visit one of the free live animal attractions, such as the Lion Habitat (▷ 26–27) at MGM Grand.

GETTING THE HEART PUMPING

Great for an adrenalin rush, brave the thrill rides atop the Stratosphere Tower (▷ 75).
The roller coaster at New York-New York (▷ 31) and Speed (▷ 74) are exhiliarating experiences.
Take to the sky in a helicopter or small plane for a bird's-eye view of the Hoover Dam (▷ 98).

The Stratosphere Tower (above); Fremont ablaze (top)

TO HIT THE SHOPPING MALLS

At Fashion Show Mall (▷ 79) you will find all the leading US department stores and lots more.
For a true smorgasbord of shopping deals, head for the outlet malls (▷ 92).
Entertainment and retail therapy go hand-in-hand at Miracle Mile (▷ 55).

DINING IN A ROMANTIC SETTING

Dine at Mon Ami Gabi (▷ 68), within view of the Bellagio fountains.
106 floors up, the revolving Top of the World (▷ 82) offers great city views and good food.
Enjoy Italian food at Canaletto (▷ 66), over-looking Venice's St. Mark's Square.

Fashion Show Mall (above right); dinner in St. Mark's Square (right)

Limos and luxury dining are part of the Las Vegas scene (below)

TO BE PAMPERED

Travel from the airport to your hotel in a stretch limousine or Hummer (▷ 119).
Check in at one of the most luxurious resorts, like the Bellagio (▷ 46).
Indulge yourself in ultimate pampering at Nurture, the Spa at Luxor (▷ 36).

DELECTABLE HOT SPOTS

Dine in restaurants created by celebrity chefs—try Bradley Ogden (▷ 66) at Caesars Palace , Michael Mina (▷ 67) at Bellagio and Thomas Keller's Bouchon (▷ 66) at the Venetian.
Take advantage of some of the city's finest French cuisine; Daniel Boulud Brasserie (▷ 82) is one of the best.
For a sweet finish to your culinary tour, have dessert at the Chocolate Swan (▷ 38) at Mandalay Place, Mandalay Bay.

HIGH-ENERGY DANCE CLUBS

Show your moves on one of the four dance floors at Studio 54 (▷ 40).
Join the super chic at Risqué (▷ 65) lost in the pulsating music.
For new innovations that will impress join the sophisticated crowd at Tryst (▷ 81).

The Grand Canal mall, what a wonderful way to shop (below)

RESORT SHOPPING

Sample unique shopping under an artificial sky at the Forum (▷ 47).
You will almost believe you are in Venice at the Grand Canal Shoppes (▷ 63).
Find a classy and distinctive collection of designer shops at the Wynn Esplanade (▷ 80).

WORLD-CLASS ENTERTAINMENT

Amazing shows, thrilling rides or a luxury spa–take your pick

See a Broadway production: *Phantom of the Opera* is still going strong at the Venetian (▷ 61).

Reserve well in advance for a close encounter with a megastar; check out the Colosseum (▷ 64) to see who's making headlines.

Be amazed by one of the many Cirque du Soleil (▷ 65) productions in town.

TO TAKE THE KIDS ALONG

Visit Circus Circus (▷ 72–73), the only gaming establishment that caters for children and adults.

The animal attractions at the Mirage (▷ 52–53) will enchant the whole family.

Children will never get bored at the Excalibur (▷ 24–25), a fantasyland of fun and games inside a sparkling castle.

NON-GAMING HOTELS

Stay within the plush sanctuary of the Four Seasons at Mandalay Bay (▷ 112).

The Alexis Park (▷ 110) provides a tranquil oasis just minutes from the action.

For state-of-the-art amenities without the gambling, the Renaissance (▷ 112) fits the bill.

You pays your money, you takes your chances (below)

SOME CASINO ACTION

Join the high rollers at the Venetian (▷ 56–57), watched over by Tiepolos and Titians.

Cocktail waitresses in togas will serve you drinks at Caesars Palace (▷ 47) while you place your bets.

Tuxedo-backed chairs set the tone at New York-New York (▷ 31), against the backdrop of the Big Apple.

Las Vegas by Area

SOUTH STRIP

CENTRAL STRIP

NORTH STRIP

DOWNTOWN

FARTHER AFIELD

Until 1990 this end of the Strip was little more than the "Welcome to Las Vegas" sign. Now the skyline is unrecognizable, with the addition of a pyramid and the Statue of Liberty, among other things.

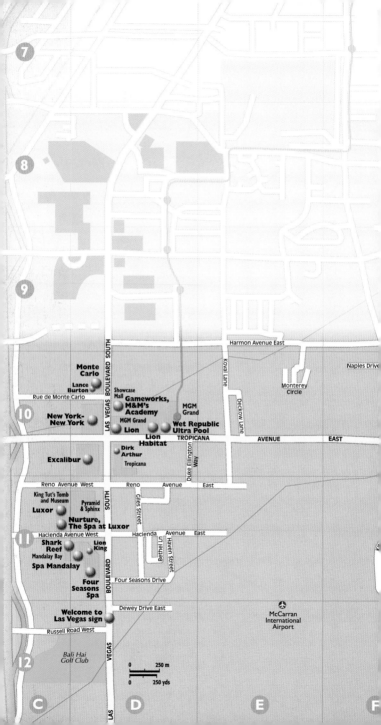

7

8

9

Harmon Avenue East

Naples Drive

Monte Carlo
Lance
Burton

LAS VEGAS BOULEVARD SOUTH

Showcase
Mall

**Gameworks,
M&M's
Academy**

MGM
Grand

Koval Lane

Monterey
Circle

Deckow Lane

Rue de Monte Carlo

10

**New York-
New York**

MGM Grand

Lion

**Lion
Habitat**

**Wet Republic
Ultra Pool**

TROPICANA

AVENUE

EAST

Excalibur

Dirk
Arthur

Tropicana

Duke Ellington Way

Reno Avenue West

Reno

Avenue

East

King Tut's Tomb
and Museum

Luxor

Pyramid
& Sphinx

**Nurture,
The Spa at Luxor**

LAS VEGAS BOULEVARD SOUTH

Giles Street

Hacienda Avenue West

Hacienda

Avenue

East

**Shark
Reef**

Mandalay Bay

**Lion
King**

Bethel Ln

Haven Street

Spa Mandalay

**Four
Seasons
Spa**

Four Seasons Drive

Dewey Drive East

**Welcome to
Las Vegas sign**

McCarran
International
Airport

Russell Road West

LAS VEGAS

Bali Hai
Golf Club

| 0 | 250 m |
| 0 | 250 yds |

C   **D**   **E**   **F**

Excalibur

HIGHLIGHTS

- Tournament of Kings
- Court Jester's Stage
- 4-D simulator rides

TIPS

- You must be at least 42in (1.06m) tall to go on the motion simulator rides.
- You will need to book well in advance for the Tournament of Kings dinner show.

All the romance and excitement of legendary medieval Europe is re-created at this sparkling castle-shaped hotel, with exciting special effects, sword fights, jousting and jugglers.

Camelot Cross the drawbridge and you enter a world where technology meets the legend of King Arthur. Inside the stone walls, stained glass and heraldic shields set the scene, and strolling performers dressed in costumes enhance the atmosphere.

Medieval Village An escalator transports you to the second floor, where you are greeted by a fire-breathing dragon. The main stage presents free shows, including juggling, puppetry and storytelling. On the lower level at the Fantasy Faire Midway there are traditional carnival attractions, state-of-the-

Fun, food and a battle royal at Tournament of Kings (left); King Arthur would feel right at home under the turrets of the Excalibur (right); illuminated at night (middle, bottom left); a feast to behold, the RoundTable buffet (bottom right)

art video games and 4-D simulator rides. Shops sell medieval-style merchandise, and there are several theme restaurants.

Tournament of Kings This enthralling show revolves around highly skilled stunts—often on horseback—high-tech special effects, wonderful costumes and a stirring musical score. King Arthur and his knights play host to other monarchs across Europe. There's a procession, followed by traditional medieval games of skill, agility, might and endurance. But when the evil Mordred attacks, amid burning fires and accompanied by a dragon, the clash of swords begins. The victor is presented with Excalibur by Merlin and the show ends with more festivities. While pulling apart their chicken dinner with greasy hands, the audience is involved in partisan support during the jousting.

THE BASICS

www.excalibur.com

⊞ D10

✉ 3850 Las Vegas Boulevard South

☎ 702/597-7777. Tournament of Kings: 702/597-7600

⏰ Tournament of Kings: Mon, Wed–Sun 6 and 8.30pm, Thu 6pm

🍴 Several cafés and restaurants

🚌 Deuce; Strip trolley

♿ Tournament of Kings: very expensive, 4-D simulator rides: inexpensive

Lion Habitat

HIGHLIGHTS

● Having a photo taken with a cub–only if there are any new additions
● Watching the trainers interact with the lions

TIPS

● The line for photos can be very long; you can bypass it and just walk through.
● The gift shop has some adorable stuffed toys for sale.

This is a remarkable place, where you can get up close to magnificent big cats in the happy knowledge that their stay in the enclosure will be only slightly longer than yours.

A temporary sojourn Anyone who has qualms about wild animals being caged for human entertainment can rest assured that the lions are brought here for just a short time from their spacious home outside the city. They belong to animal trainer Keith Evans, who makes the trip three times a day to ensure that no cat is in the enclosure for longer than six hours.

Surrounded by lions The three-level structure, reaching a height of more than 35ft (10m), is similar in concept to the walk-through tunnels

Have a rip-roaring time observing these magnificent creatures in their glass enclosure

you'll find in big aquariums. You will see the animals close up, and can study their every move with perfect clarity as they prowl on either side and even stride across the tunnel roof above your head—and all that separates you is a thick layer of the toughest strengthened glass available. The Lion Habitat has been laid out to resemble the natural landscape the cats would know in the wild, including indigenous foliage, rocks, four separate waterfalls and a pond.

Raised in captivity One of the most famous lions of all time was Metro, whose roar announced every MGM Studio production. Three of his descendants—Goldie, Metro and Baby Lion—are among the collection of more than two dozen big cats, all of which have been raised in captivity by Evans and his wife at their 8-acre (3ha) estate.

THE BASICS

www.mgmgrand.com

✚ D10

✉ MGM Grand, 3799 Las Vegas Boulevard South

☎ 702/891-7777

🕐 Daily 11–10

🍴 Cafés and restaurants at MGM Grand

🚇 MGM Grand

🚌 Deuce

🎟 Free

Luxor

It may be disconcerting that the Luxor's interior has been stripped of its Egyptian theme to make way for a trendy new image, but don't despair, two exciting new exhibitions more than compensate.

Egyptian roots Although things have changed inside at the Luxor, the gigantic black-glass pyramid, complete with a massive 10-floor replica sphinx at the entrance, still dominates—which is no surprise as it is the main hotel building. An intense narrow beam shoots out from the top of the pyramid; claimed to be the strongest beam of light in the world, on a clear night it is visible from outer space.

***Titanic* docks at Luxor** *Titanic*: The Artifact Exhibition takes you on an emotional journey back

The infamous sphinx and exterior of Luxor (top left, below middle right) are all that remain of its Egyptian theme. New additions to the hotel include the fascinating Titanic Exhibition (below left) with genuine items from the ship and interactive displays

in time to experience the ill-fated ship's maiden voyage. On display are hundreds of authentic objects recovered from *Titanic's* final resting place. A reconstructed ship's bow utilizes a moving lifeboat to gain access on board. Walk through room creations, share in the dramatic stories of the passengers and crew and experience the feel of an iceberg, which set the stage for one of history's greatest tragedies.

Come see what's inside Bodies…The Exhibition is an enlightening opportunity to see the inner workings of our bodies through preserved, full-size human bodies, plus more than 260 organs and partial body specimens. This must-see attraction is a groundbreaking venture for Las Vegas—a fairly serious experience that will leave you with many lasting thoughts.

THE BASICS

www.luxor.com

🔀 D11

✉ 3900 Las Vegas Boulevard South

☎ 702/262-4444

🎫 *Titanic* and Bodies exhibitions: daily 10–10

🍴 Several cafés and restaurants

🚌 Deuce

♿ *Titanic* and Bodies exhibitions: expensive

Liberace Museum

What a showman (left); welcome to Liberace's world (middle); a prized Rolls-Royce (right)

THE BASICS

www.liberace.org

🏠 H10

✉ 1775 East Tropicana Avenue, at Spencer

☎ 702/798-5595

🕐 Tue–Sat 10–5, Sun 12–4

🍴 Café

🚌 201

💵 Moderate

HIGHLIGHTS

● Concert piano collection
● Rolls-Royce collection
● Costumes, including a black diamond mink cape and the famous red, white and blue hot-pants suit
● Candelabra ring
● Precious stone collection
● Re-creation of Palm Springs bedroom

Outrageous and ostentatious—a testament to bad taste and kitsch. This description could easily be used as a slogan for Las Vegas city, but here it refers to just one collection, the incredible Liberace Museum.

Setting the scene From the moment you see the fluorescent pink entrance sign, you are drawn into the world of one of the most extraordinary entertainers of the 20th century. This shrine to the legend of "Mr Showmanship" is as outrageous as Liberace himself. The museum, the legacy of the world's highest-paid musician, was founded by Liberace in 1977 as a non-profit organization. On show are vintage pianos and cars, exuberant costumes, glitzy jewelry and a host of memorabilia.

From classical beginnings Born in the US in 1919 of Italian/Polish parents, Wladziu Liberace had a classical training and made his debut with the Chicago Symphony at the age of 14. In 1955 he opened at the Riviera as the highest-paid entertainer in the city's history, his flamboyant style always attracting attention. He died in 1987.

Antiques to kitsch To the rippling tones of Liberace's keyboard artistry you can view an amazing collection of pianos, including rare antiques. Check out the rhinestone-encrusted Baldwin grand and Liberace's favorite, covered entirely in glittering mirror squares. See the superb bejeweled Rolls-Royces, sequined, feathered and rhinestone-studded costumes and a glittering array of jewelry, including the trademark candelabra ring.

New York-New York

See the sights of the Big Apple in a fraction of the time needed to explore the real thing. The Statue of Liberty, Brookyn Bridge, the Chrysler Building—they are all here.

New York in miniature This resort hotel depicts the New York skyline through scaled-down replicas—about one-third of the actual size—of famous city landmarks. The Statue of Liberty sits side by side with skyscrapers such as the Empire State Building and a 300ft-long (91m) version of the Brooklyn Bridge. At the base of the Statue of Liberty replica is a tribute to the 9/11 heroes. Among the cherished items on display are T-shirts bearing fire station and police department insignia and letters from firefighters.

White-knuckle ride A thrilling roller coaster twists, loops and dives at speeds of up to 67mph (97kph) around the skyscrapers to a height of 203ft (62m). Your whole world literally turns upside down and inside out when the train drops 144ft (44m). This ride was the first ever to introduce the "heartline" twist and dive move, where riders experience weightlessness—the train rolls 180 degrees, suspending its passengers 86ft (26m) above the casino roof, before taking a sudden dive.

Behind the scenes The hotel's art deco lobby is set against representations of Times Square, Little Italy and Wall Street, and the casino is modeled on Central Park. A selection of restaurants and shops also follows the theme.

THE BASICS

www.nynyhotelcasino.com
🕂 D10
✉ 3790 Las Vegas Boulevard South
☎ 702/740-6969
🕐 Rollercoaster: Sun–Thu 11–11, Fri, Sat 11–midnight
🍴 Several cafés and restaurants
🚇 MGM Grand
🚌 Deuce
♿ Manhattan Express: moderate
❓ You must be 54in (1.38m) to ride the roller coaster

HIGHLIGHTS

- Roller coaster
- Statue of Liberty
- Brooklyn Bridge
- Tribute to 9/11 heroes

Shark Reef

TOP 25

HIGHLIGHTS

- Sharks up to 12ft (3.5m) long
- Back Reef Tunnel
- Talking to the naturalists
- Touch pool
- Golden crocodiles

TIP

- A self-guiding audio tour is included in the price, with cards to help you identify the fish.

A hundred different species of shark, plus other magnificent aquatic creatures, can be encountered close up in the imaginatively re-created marine environments of this aquarium.

Massive tanks Shark Reef covers more than 91,000sq ft (8,450sq m) and its tanks—arranged in 14 main exhibits—contain an incredible 1.6 million gallons (7.2 million liters) of mineral-rich reconstituted sea water. It is home to more than 2,000 species of marine creatures—not only the sharks, but also sea turtles, reptiles and fish.

The major exhibits In Treasure Bay, a sunken ship sits on the bed of a lagoon, circled by four kinds of shark. Shoals of snapper and jack dart around, in contrast to the laid-back gliding of the two green

Visitors marvel at the marine life in Mandalay Bay—lionfish (top left), bonnethead shark (top middle), stingray (below right)—to name a few

sea turtles. The experience of diving on a coral reef is re-created in the Back Reef Tunnel, whose water is full of bright tropical fish to the left, right and above you, and there is every probability of coming nose to nose with bonnethead sharks. Elsewhere, you will see rays skimming through the water or resting on the ocean floor.

Reptiles, amphibians and jungle flora Rare golden crocodiles inhabit the Crocodile Habitat (the only place in the western hemisphere where you can see them), and in the Lizard Lounge there are huge water monitor lizards up to 9ft (2.7m) in length. The Serpents and Dragons exhibit, separated from curious onlookers by only a pool of water, houses venomous snakes and the Australian Arowana dragon fish. The Temple exhibits offer a refreshing rain-forest experience.

THE BASICS

www.sharkreef.com
✚ C11
✉ Mandalay Bay, 3950 Las Vegas Boulevard South
☎ 702/632-4555
🕐 Sun–Thu 10–7, Fri–Sat 10–9
🍴 Cafés and restaurants at Mandalay Bay
🚌 Deuce
♿ Moderate

More to See

DIRK ARTHUR: XTREME MAGIC

www.tropicanalv.com
It's magic to the extreme, with revolutionary magician Dirk Arthur's fast-paced show interweaving dance, breathtaking magic and exotic animals.

➕ D10 ✉ Tropicana, 3801 Las Vegas Boulevard South ☎ 702/739-2222 🕐 Sat–Thu 2 and 4pm 🚇 MGM Grand 🚌 Deuce ✋ Expensive

FOUR SEASONS SPA

www.fourseasons.com/lasvegas
An exquisite facility for the ultimate pampering. Treatments include facials, body scrubs, massages and mud treatments, and there are two private spa suites, with sauna, steam room, whirlpool tub and massage table. The fitness suite includes weights and cardiovascular equipment, saunas and Jacuzzis, and there's a jogging track through the beautiful grounds.

➕ D11 ✉ Four Seasons, 3960 Las Vegas Boulevard South ☎ 702/632-5000 🕐 Daily 8–8 🚌 Deuce

GAMEWORKS

www.gameworks.com
A creation from movie mogul Steven Spielberg that is the ultimate in interactive, virtual-reality arcade games; it is geared mostly to teenagers.

➕ D10 ✉ Showcase Mall, 3785 Las Vegas Boulevard South ☎ 702/432-4263 🕐 Sun–Thu 10am–midnight, Fri, Sat 10am–1am 🚇 MGM Grand 🚌 Deuce ✋ Admission free; individual activities inexpensive

LANCE BURTON: MASTER MAGICIAN

www.montecarlo.com
A fascinating display of the illusionist's art, plus traditional sleight-of-hand tricks that leave the audiences gasping. A good family show.

➕ D10 ✉ Monte Carlo, 3770 Las Vegas Boulevard South ☎ 702/730-7160 🕐 Tue–Sat 7pm (also Tue, Sat 10pm) 🚌 Deuce ✋ Very expensive

THE LION KING

www.mandalaybay.com
Opened May 2009, The Lion King is

Sheer heaven at the Four Seasons Spa

Lance Burton conjures up a magic moment

the first Disney production to play in this gambling Mecca (a gamble in itself). The show reigns as one of the most popular productions around the globe, and the Mandalay Bay's production follows this successful format, with all of the same spectacular music, sets and costumes. An amazing show.

🚺 D11 ✉ Mandalay Bay, 3950 Las Vegas Boulevard South ☎ 702/632-7777 🕐 Mon–Thu 8pm, Sat–Sun 4 and 8pm 🚌 Deuce 💵 Very Expensive

THE LION OUTSIDE MGM

Unlike its live counterparts inside the MGM Grand (▷ 26–27), this sedentary lion is made of bronze, is 45ft (14m) tall and weighs in at 100,000lb (45,360kg). It represents MGM Studios' signature lion, Metro.

🚺 D10 ✉ MGM Grand, 3799 Las Vegas Boulevard South 🚇 MGM Grand 🚌 Deuce

M&M'S ACADEMY

www.mms.com

An interactive retail complex over four floors with M&M's brand merchandise items, plus a 3-D movie theater, an M&M's Racing Team store and a wall covered in a multitude of different colored plain and peanut M&Ms.

🚺 D10 ✉ Showcase Mall, 3785 Las Vegas Boulevard South ☎ 702/736-7611 🕐 Sun–Thu 9am–11pm, Fri, Sat 9–midnight 🚇 MGM Grand 🚌 Deuce 💵 Admission free; movie inexpensive

MARJORIE BARRICK MUSEUM OF NATURAL HISTORY

http://hrc.nevada.edu/museum

Less than 3 miles (5km) from the Strip on the university campus is this excellent museum devoted to the Native Americans of the region, the wildlife and also the history of ancient Mesoamerica.

🚺 G10 ✉ 4505 South Maryland Parkway ☎ 702/895-3381 🕐 Mon–Fri 8–4.45, Sat 10–2 🚌 109 💵 Free–donation

MONTE CARLO

www.montecarlo.com

Chandeliered domes, ornate fountains and gaslit promenades set the scene at this resort hotel modeled on the Place

The sweet taste of success at M&M's

Monte Carlo or bust

du Casino in Monte Carlo. The master illusionist Lance Burton (▷ 35), has been here for a number of years.
✚ D10 ✉ 3770 Las Vegas Boulevard South ☎ 702/730-7777 🚌 Deuce

NURTURE, THE SPA AT LUXOR
www.luxor.com
Soothe your tired body in beautiful surroundings. A whole range of exercise equipment—treadmills, bicycles, weight machines, climbing machines—is available here, along with such treatments as body wraps, body scrubs, massages, hydrotherapy and facials. There are tanning beds, too.
✚ C11 ✉ Luxor, 3900 Las Vegas Boulevard South ☎ 702/730-5724 🕐 Daily 24 hours 🚌 Deuce; Strip trolley

SPA MANDALAY
www.mandalaybay.com
This opulent facility has picture windows with a wonderful view over the hotel's lagoon and gardens. In addition to traditional treatments, there is a range of more exotic techniques, including ayurvedic relaxation and

Swedish massage, while amenities include whirlpools with waterfalls, saunas and Swedish showers.
✚ D11 ✉ Mandalay Bay, 3950 Las Vegas Boulevard South ☎ 702/632-7777 🕐 Daily 8–9 🚌 Deuce

"WELCOME TO FABULOUS LAS VEGAS" SIGN
Designed in 1959, this famous sign welcomes you as you enter Las Vegas at the south end of the Strip.
✚ D12 ✉ 5200 Las Vegas Boulevard South 🚌 Deuce; 116, 104

WET REPUBLIC ULTRA POOL
www.mgmgrand.com
Forget nightlife, this is the latest Vegas craze—daylife. Grab your most fashionable swimwear and visit the MGM for the ultimate pool experience. Here you will find two state-of-the-art saltwater pools, eight individual pools and spas, party cabanas and comfortable loungers. Let the party begin.
✚ D10 ✉ MGM Grand, 3799 Las Vegas Boulevard South ☎ 702/891-3563 🕐 Daily 11am–dusk Ⓜ MGM Grand 🚌 Deuce

Just in case you need to be reminded where you are

Come inside and spoil yourself at Spa Mandalay

Shopping

CASTLE WALK

Well and truly carrying on the medieval theme, this mall includes a range of gift shops selling magic tricks and accoutrements, medieval replica swords and shields (and the occasional suit of armor).

➕ D10 ✉ Excalibur, 3850 Las Vegas Boulevard South ☎ 702/597-7850 🚇 Deuce

CHOCOLATE SWAN

www.mandalaybay.com

This long-established family-owned bakery and chocolate shop show-cases creations made onsite and wonderful desserts, made with the finest ingredients.

➕ D11 ✉ Mandalay Place, Mandalay Bay, 3950 Las Vegas Boulevard South ☎ 702/632-7777 🚇 Deuce

HOUDINI MAGIC

Every 15 minutes until midnight you can watch live magic shows, and then buy your own magic tricks from the selection of sleight-of-hand tricks available for sale.

➕ D10 ✉ MGM Grand, 3799 Las Vegas Boulevard South ☎ 702/891-7777 🚇 MGM Grand 🚇 Deuce

LIBERACE MUSEUM GIFT STORE

www.liberace.org

For ardent Liberace fans, among the souvenirs for sale are Liberace-theme items, CDs, music-related books, giftware, stationery and jewelry.

➕ H10 ✉ 1775 Tropicana Avenue East ☎ 702/798-5595 🚇 201

M&M'S ACADEMY

www.mms.com

A tourist attraction as well as a candy store, this place has a huge selection of well-known confectionery brands, including a vast array of liqueur-filled chocolates and, of course, M&M's.

➕ D10 ✉ Showcase Mall, 3785 Las Vegas Boulevard South ☎ 702/736-7611 🚇 Deuce

MANDALAY PLACE

A sky bridge connecting Mandalay Bay with the Luxor is home to a number of superior retailers. These include top designer names in men's and women's fashion, renowned jewelery stores and other specialties.

➕ D11 ✉ Mandalay Bay, 3950 Las Vegas Boulevard South ☎ 702/632-7777 🚇 Deuce

PEARL FACTORY

See how pearls are cultured before you make your decision, and have them mounted in the setting of your choice. Hawaiian heirloom jewelry is also displayed.

➕ D10 ✉ MGM Grand, 3799 Las Vegas Boulevard South ☎ 702/891-0344 🚇 MGM Grand 🚇 Deuce

PEARL MOON BOUTIQUE

It's a bit on the pricey side, but the selection of swimwear, hats, sunglasses and sandals here is better quality than you'll find at other shops on the Strip.

➕ D11 ✉ Mandalay Bay, 3950 Las Vegas Boulevard South ☎ 702/632-7777 🚇 Deuce

STREET OF DREAMS

A modest mall with clothing boutiques, plus the fascinating Lance Burton Magic Shop, with souvenirs and magic tricks to remind you of the master illusionist's show (▷ 35).

➕ D10 ✉ Monte Carlo, 3770 Las Vegas Boulevard South ☎ 702/730-7777 🚇 Deuce

---

HOTEL SHOPPING

You will find many familiar stores in hotel malls, such as Gap, Victoria's Secret, Tommy Bahama and Levi's Original, and the classier places will have designer boutiques like Prada and Hermès, too. You won't find the big department stores here, but you'll be able to buy a good range of items, including more mundane requirements such as toiletries, cosmetics and magazines. Souvenirs may include pieces that reflect the hotel's theme, or merchandise from the permanent shows and visiting entertainers.

Entertainment and Nightlife

BALI HAI GOLF CLUB
www.balihaigolfclub.com
A South Pacific theme pervades throughout this 18-hole course, with outcrops of volcanic rock, groups of palm trees and white sand in the bunkers.
✛ D12 ✉ 5160 Las Vegas Boulevard ☎ 702/597-2400 🚌 Deuce; 104, 116

BODY ENGLISH
www.bodyenglish.com
Cavelike booths and innovative design create elegance with an edge at this buzzing two-tiered dance club. The energetic music avoids the endless techno drone.
✛ F10 ✉ Hard Rock Hotel, 4455 Paradise Road ☎ 702/693-4000 🚌 108

CELEBRATION LOUNGE
www.tropicanalv.com
Entertaining singing bartenders offer up anything from Frank Sinatra to Patsy Cline and still find time to serve some of the best margaritas in the city.
✛ D10 ✉ Tropicana, 3801 Las Vegas Boulevard South ☎ 702/739-2222 🚇 MGM Grand 🚌 Deuce

COYOTE UGLY
www.coyoteuglysaloon.com
If you enjoyed the movie or have visited the New York original, you'll love it here. It's a fun Southern-style saloon with wild bartenders who dance on the bar.

✛ D10 ✉ New York-New York, 3790 Las Vegas Boulevard South ☎ 702/740 6330 🚌 Deuce

GRAND GARDEN ARENA
www.mgmgrand.com
This is one of the biggest venues in town, hosting huge events ranging from top entertainers to world championship boxing.
✛ D10 ✉ MGM Grand, 3799 Las Vegas Boulevard South ☎ 702/891-7777 🚇 MGM Grand 🚌 Deuce

HOLLYWOOD THEATER
www.mgmgrand.com
MGM's smaller venue hosting world-class

TICKET INFORMATION

The popular long-running shows and the new ones sell out quickly, so it's advisable to make reservations. Call the relevant hotel or check out its website, which will have a reservation facility. Otherwise, shows can be reserved through TicketMaster (www.ticket master.com). Reservations are taken for long-running shows up to 30 days in advance; limited-time concerts or sporting events such as boxing matches can be reserved three months in advance. Note that shows can close with little notice so it is always best to check to avoid disappointment.

performers—including Tom Jones and David Copperfield—also puts on top-line comedy acts.
✛ D10 ✉ MGM Grand, 3799 Las Vegas Boulevard South ☎ 702/891-7777 🚇 MGM Grand 🚌 Deuce

HOUSE OF BLUES
www.mandalaybay.com
Bringing New Orleans to Las Vegas, this superb, 1,500-seat venue is on three levels and features such big-name stars as B. B. King and Brian Ferry. There's great food, including the popular Sunday Gospel Brunch. Check out the unusual artworks, too.
✛ D11 ✉ Mandalay Bay, 3950 Las Vegas Boulevard South ☎ 702/632-7600 🚌 Deuce

THE JOINT
www.hardrockhotel.com
One of Vegas' hottest venues, with a capacity of 1,400, bringing in cutting-edge bands worthy of the Hard Rock image.
✛ F10 ✉ Hard Rock Hotel, 4455 Paradise Road ☎ 702/693-4000 🚌 108

LAX
www.laxthenightclub.com
A huge dramatic two-story space with dramatic spiral staircases, oversized mirrors and chandeliers that attract a cool young crowd. Top DJs play from a raised platform through an unrivaled sound system to the swanky dance floor below.

🚏 D11 ✉ Luxor, 3900 Las Vegas Boulevard South ☎ 702/262-4000 🚍 Deuce

MANDALAY BAY EVENTS CENTER
www.mandalaybay.com
This major venue hosts big-name concerts and sporting events. On one night, usually in June, it is transformed into a gigantic nightclub for the "Summer of Love" event.
🚏 D11 ✉ Mandalay Bay, 3950 Las Vegas Boulevard South ☎ 702/632-7777 🚍 Deuce

MIX LOUNGE
www.mandalaybay.com
Mix a seductive blend of music played by savvy DJs, great cocktails, breathtaking views from 64 floors up and you have one of the most stylish and fashionable hotspots on the Strip.
🚏 D11 ✉ Mandalay Bay, 3950 Las Vegas Boulevard South ☎ 702/632-9500 🚍 Deuce

THE PUB
www.montecarlo.com
After extensive modification, out go the huge copper barrels that typified the Monte Carlo Brew Pub and in comes a new contemporary look and a new name to go with it.
🚏 D10 ✉ Monte Carlo, 3770 Las Vegas Boulevard South ☎ 702/730-7777 🎧 Mon–Thu 11am–2am, Fri

11am–4am, Sat 10am–4am, Sun 10am–2am 🚍 Deuce

RUMJUNGLE
www.mandalaybay.com
This sizzling hot club has a Caribbean theme and some breathtaking features—acrobats in harnesses launch themselves across the ceiling and there is a wall of flames and a waterfall.
🚏 D11 ✉ Mandalay Bay, 3950 Las Vegas Boulevard South ☎ 702/632-7777 🚍 Deuce

DRESS CODES
Most, if not all, of the nightclubs listed here impose quite a strict dress code, so it's a good idea to check what is acceptable beforehand. Men will have more trouble than women when it comes to what they are wearing: jeans and sneakers are guaranteed to keep hopefuls out of any club. Women are also more likely than men to get in when there are long lines. You can get onto the VIP list if you know someone who works at the club, or if you have spent a lot in the casino. Otherwise, join the line outside the door (about an hour before opening time at the most popular places) and hope for the best. Cover charges, where they exist, are usually less than $20, and may be at different rates for men and women.

SOPRANO'S LAST SUPPER
www.sopranoslast supper.com
An interactive spoof on the famous hit TV series, The Sopranos. Plenty of action, singing and dancing and a first-class Italian dinne to indulge in, but don't expect to stay in your seat all evening.
🚏 D10 ✉ Tropicana, 3801 Las Vegas Boulevard South ☎ 702/733-8669; 800/829-9034 🚇 MGM Grand 🎭 Shows Tue–Sun 7pm 🚍 Deuce

STUDIO 54
www.mgmgrand.com
Popular with celebrities, this is high-energy club. A replica of the famous 1970s original in New York, complete with good time vibe.
🚏 D10 ✉ MGM Grand, 3799 Las Vegas Boulevard South ☎ 702/891-7254 🚇 MGM Grand 🚍 Deuce

THOMAS & MACK CENTER/SAM BOYD STADIUM
www.unlvtickets.com
State-of-the-art multipurpose arena that stages world-class entertainment and major national sports events, with a seating capacity of 19,511. From monster truck racing, boxing and show jumping to music concerts, rodeo, basketball and ice shows.
🚏 G10 ✉ University of Nevada, South Maryland Parkway ☎ 702/895-3761 🚍 109

Restaurants

PRICES

Prices are approximate, based on a 3-course meal for one person.
$$$ over $50
$$ $20–$50
$ under $20

AUREOLE ($$$)

www.mandalaybay.com
This restaurant has big windows, glass-covered waterfalls and a massive award-winning wine tower. American dishes dominate the first-class menu here.

➕ D11 ✉ Mandalay Bay, 3950 Las Vegas Boulevard South ☎ 702/632-7401
🕐 Daily 6–10.30 🚌 Deuce

BAYSIDE ($$)

www.mandalaybay.com
Floor-to-ceiling windows here give sweeping views of the tropical lagoon outside. Although the buffet is not over-large, the cuisine is very good, with excellent salads, hearty meats and one of the better dessert selections, all made on the premises.

➕ D11 ✉ Mandalay Bay, 3950 Las Vegas Boulevard South ☎ 702/632-7402
🕐 Daily 7–2.30, 4.45–10
🚌 Deuce

BORDER GRILL ($$)

www.mandalaybay.com
Great Mexican home cooking in a lively setting. Lunch on spicy baby back ribs on the patio or get a take-out taco.

➕ D11 ✉ Mandalay Bay, 3950 Las Vegas Boulevard South ☎ 702/632-7403
🕐 Mon–Thu 11.30–10, Fri 11.30–11, Sat 11–11, Sun 11–10
🚌 Deuce

CATHOUSE ($$)

www.cathouselv.com
A classy hybrid of a seductive restaurant, orchestrated by celebrity chef Kerry Simon, and Burlesque-style lounge. The eclectic menu features shared small-plate fusion dishes.

➕ D11 ✉ Luxor, 3900 Las Vegas Boulevard South
☎ 702/262-4852
🕐 Mon–Sun 6pm–11pm
🚌 Deuce

CHARLIE PALMER STEAK ($$$)

www.fourseasons.com/lasvegas
Subdued gleaming woodwork and bronze, and an exclusive atmosphere, set the scene for a meal that might include charcoal-grilled filet mignon or steamed halibut.

➕ D11 ✉ Four Seasons, 3960 Las Vegas Boulevard South ☎ 702/632-5000
🕐 Daily 5.30–10.15
🚌 Deuce

CHINA GRILL ($$$)

www.mandalaybay.com
Come with a group of friends or family and prepare to splurge on the massive portions served up in this imaginative Asian restaurant.

➕ D11 ✉ Mandalay Bay, 3950 Las Vegas Boulevard South ☎ 702/632-7404
🕐 Daily 5.30–midnight
🚌 Deuce

CRAFTSTEAK ($$$)

www.mgmgrand.com
Beautifully prepared hand-selected beef from small farms and artisan producers.

➕ D10 ✉ MGM Grand, 3799 Las Vegas Boulevard South ☎ 702/891-7318
🕐 Sun–Thu 5.30–10, Fri 5.30–10.30, Sat 5–10.30
🚌 MGM Grand 🚌 Deuce

EMERIL'S ($$$)

www.mgmgrand.com
This is a re-creation of Emeril Lagasse's sophisticated New Orleans restaurant. The menu includes barbecued shrimp, veal sirloin, and sumptuous banana cream pie.

➕ D10 ✉ MGM Grand, 3799 Las Vegas Boulevard South ☎ 702/891-7374

A NEW IMAGE

At one time, the only culinary experience for which Las Vegas was famous was the opportunity to stuff yourself with as much food as you could for a very reasonable price. Now the city has become renowned for the amount of choice available, with every kind of cuisine and style to suit every budget. For special-occasion dining in sumptuous surroundings, the best hotel restaurants are at the Bellagio, Mandalay Bay and the Venetian.

SOUTH STRIP · **RESTAURANTS**

🕐 Daily 11–2.30, 5.30–10.30
🚇 MGM Grand 🚌 Deuce

IL FORNAIO PANETTERIA ($)

www.nynyhotelcasino.com
It's worth making a
special journey to this
Italian bakery café just for
its espresso-mocha scone
with chocolate chunks.
➕ D10 ✉ New York-New
York, 3790 Las Vegas
Boulevard South ☎ 702/740-
6403 🕐 Daily 7.30–midnight
🚇 MGM Grand 🚌 Deuce

JOËL ROBUCHON ($$$)

www.mgmgrand.com
Robuchon's reputation
for the highest standards
is upheld here at the
MGM. The sophisticated
16-course menu is an
experience or if you pre-
fer a scaled-down version,
choose the six-course
tasting menu.
➕ D10 ✉ MGM Grand,
3799 Las Vegas Boulevard
South ☎ 702/891-7925
🕐 Sun–Thu 5.30–10, Fri–Sat
5.30–10.30 🚇 MGM Grand
🚌 Deuce

NOBHILL TAVERN ($$$)

www.mgmgrand.com
A taste of San Francisco
is brought to Vegas by
celebrity chef Michael
Mina. Try any of the
five kinds of whipped
potatoes, Tasmanian
ocean trout, lobster pot
pie or beef rib eye.
➕ D10 ✉ MGM Grand,
3767 Las Vegas Boulevard

South ☎ 702/891-7337
🕐 Sun–Thu 5.30–10, Fri, Sat
5.30–10.30 🚇 MGM Grand
🚌 Deuce

NOODLE SHOP ($)

www.mandalaybay.com
The food here really
hits the spot when you
need sustenance at any
time of day. It offers
over 20 kinds of noodle-
and-rice dishes, served
hot and at lightning
speed, plus barbecued
meat dishes.
➕ D11 ✉ Mandalay Bay,
3950 Las Vegas Boulevard
South ☎ 702/632-7934
🕐 Sun–Thu 11–11, Fri–Sat
11am–1am 🚌 Deuce

CHILD-FRIENDLY

Apart from the countless fast-
food establishments selling
hot dogs, burgers and pizzas,
Las Vegas has many more
options to prevent your kids
from going hungry. Buffets
enable them to pick and
choose what they like, and
most have an ice-cream
machine that you can use to
blackmail them into eating
their greens. Theme restaurants that children will love
include the Rainforest Café at
the MGM Grand (✉ 3799
Las Vegas Boulevard South
☎ 702/891-8580; www.
rainforestcafe.com
🕐 Sun–Thu 8am–11pm, Fri,
Sat 8am–midnight), with jungle foliage, waterfalls, robotic
animals and thunderstorms.

RED SQUARE ($$)

www.mandalaybay.com
Wash latkes and blinis
down with vodka, or
choose US and French
dishes, in this Russian-
theme restaurant where
the headless statue of
Lenin, the red-velvet
drapes and the fake
Communist propaganda
give the game away.
➕ D11 ✉ Mandalay Bay,
3950 Las Vegas Boulevard
South ☎ 702/632-7407
🕐 Daily 5–10.30 🚌 Deuce

TOTO'S ($)

This family-run restaurant
serves enormous help-
ings of good Mexican
food. It's popular with
locals who welcome the
good value.
➕ H10 ✉ 2055 East
Tropicana Avenue ☎ 702/
895-7923 🕐 Mon–Thu
11–10, Fri–Sat 11–11, Sun
9.30–10 🚌 201

VERANDAH HIGH TEA ($$)

www.fourseasons.com/lasvegas
It's quite a surprise to
find that great British
institution, afternoon
tea, in the middle of
Vegas. Sandwiches,
scones with cream and
jam, French pastries, plus
a selection of fine teas.
Piano music completes
the elegant scene.
Reservations required.
➕ D11 ✉ Four Seasons,
3960 Las Vegas Boulevard
South ☎ 702/632-5000
🕐 Mon–Thu 3–4pm
🚌 Deuce

With no less than seven theme hotels, this section of the Strip is capable of transporting you into a world of make-believe, with fire-spewing volcanoes and magical fountains.

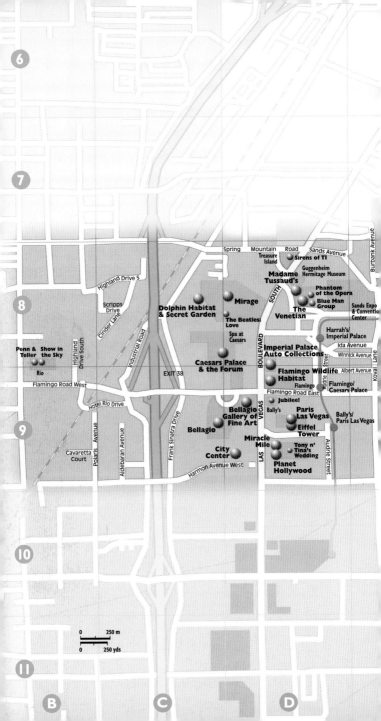

Spring Mountain Road
Sands Avenue
Burbank Avenue

Treasure Island
Sirens of TI

Madame Tussaud's
Guggenheim Hermitage Museum

Phantom of the Opera
Blue Man Group

Mirage
SOUTH
The Venetian

Dolphin Habitat & Secret Garden

Sands Expo & Convention Center

Highland Drive S

Scripps Drive

Cinder Lane

Industrial Road

The Beatles: Love

Spa at Caesars

BOULEVARD

Harrah's
Imperial Palace

Penn & Teller   Show in the Sky

Imperial Palace Auto Collections

Ida Avenue
Winnick Avenue

Koval Lane

Rio

Highland Drive South

EXIT 38

Caesars Palace & the Forum

Flamingo Wildlife Habitat

Albert Avenue

Audrie Street

Flamingo Road West

Hotel Rio Drive

Flamingo Road East

Flamingo/
Caesars Palace

VEGAS

Jubilee!

Bally's

Paris Las Vegas

Bally's/
Paris Las Vegas

Cavaretta Court

Polaris Avenue

Aldebaran Avenue

Frank Sinatra Drive

Bellagio Gallery of Fine Art

Bellagio

Eiffel Tower

LAS

Miracle Mile

Tony n' Tina's Wedding

City Center

Audrie Street

Harmon Avenue West

Planet Hollywood

0   250 m
0   250 yds

6
7
8
9
10
11

B   C   D

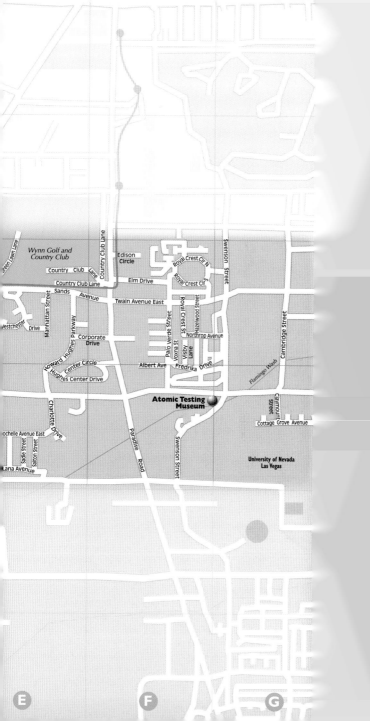

Bellagio

Showtime at Bellagio (left); a Chinese dragon greets guests (middle); the hotel pool (right)

HIGHLIGHTS

● Fountain show
● Gallery of Fine Art
● Botanical garden
● The lobby

The Italianate image for this $1.6 billion hotel, deemed to be one of the most opulent resorts in the world, was inspired by the village of Bellagio on the shores of Italy's Lake Como.

A touch of class A 10-acre (4ha) man-made lake at the front of the hotel sets the stage for the elegance, art and grandeur that awaits you inside. The dazzling front lobby has an 18ft (5.5m) ceiling with a chandelier of glass flowers suspended in the middle, designed by glass sculptor Dale Chihuly. All this splendor is enhanced by the wonderful botanical garden, set under a glass atrium.

Fountains at Bellagio During the choreographed, computer-controlled fountain show, millions of gallons of water are sprayed to heights of 240ft (73m) above the hotel's massive lake. The system uses individually programmed water jets and atomizing nozzles that create an atmospheric fog on the lake; some jets can change the direction of the water, giving a dancing effect. The show is further enhanced by the integrated illumination that comes into play after dark, and by the audio system, with music ranging from Pavarotti to Sinatra.

So much The hotel's casino oozes sophistication, its slot machines encased in marble and wood. Bellagio is proud of its Gallery of Fine Art (▶ 59), and its magnificent theater was styled after the Paris Opera specifically for Cirque du Soleil's "O" (▶ 65). The extravagant glass-enclosed shopping mall (▶ 64) has an array of exclusive boutiques.

Hail Caesars, in all its glory (left); the Forum, famous for its incredible fountains (right)

Caesars Palace and the Forum

So you're in Las Vegas, and the thing you most want to do is spend a day shopping for Italian-designer chic surrounded by the historic buildings of ancient Rome? No problem. It's all here at Caesars Palace.

Classical architecture You could easily believe that you have been transported into the Italian capital, amid architecture that spans the period from 300BC to AD1700. The grounds are filled with reproductions of Roman statues, marble columns and colonnades, and toga-clad cocktail waitresses and costumed centurions tend to your every need in the exciting casino.

The Forum Visit the phenomenal shopping concourse, the Forum. Wander in and out of such stores as Versace and Roberto Cavalli or eat at one of the many restaurants. An artificial sky overhead gives the illusion that 24 hours have passed in just one hour. Every hour the Festival of Fountains springs into action, when statues come to life, special effects kick in, and you are entertained by characters from Roman mythology. In the Roman Great Hall, more special effects and animatronics combine to portray the struggle to rule Atlantis, with the backdrop of a massive marine aquarium.

Star-studded performances The 4,000-seat Colosseum has hosted big-name shows, including Cher and Elton John. Other attractions include a 3-D IMAX motion simulator where three-dimensional images and sound systems offer a unique experience.

THE BASICS

www.caesarspalace.com

➕ C8–D8

✉ 3570 Las Vegas Boulevard South

☎ 702/731-7110. The Forum 702/893-4800

🕐 Festival of Fountains/ Atlantis show: daily every hour 10am–11pm

🍴 Several cafés and restaurants

🚊 Flamingo/Caesars

🚌 Deuce

♿ Festival of Fountains/ Atlantis show: free

HIGHLIGHTS

● Shops in the Forum
● Festival of Fountains and Atlantis show
● A performance at the Colosseum

Dolphin Habitat and the Secret Garden

HIGHLIGHTS

● Watching the dolphins frolic
● Seeing the cats close up
● If you're lucky, being there when a baby dolphin has just been born

TIPS

● You can stay as long as you like, so be patient and you are more likely to observe a special moment.
● If they aren't doing it already, ask the keepers to play ball with the dolphins.

Here you can be entertained by marine mammals playing in their natural environment or get close up with some of the rarest and most exotic animals in the world, all in one afternoon.

Dolphins at play To the rear of the Mirage, the Dolphin Habitat's intent is to provide a happy and nurturing environment for Atlantic bottlenose dolphins and increase public awareness and the commitment to protect and conserve marine animals in general. Watch these amazing mammals frolic across a shimmering lagoon or below from the viewing gallery, and learn more about marine mammals on a 15-minute tour. The dolphins breed regularly, so you might be fortunate enough to see a baby at play. All the dolphins have names and respond to their keepers' instructions.

The dolphins come out to play; you can see Siegfried and Roy's famous tigers in their habitat inside the Mirage at the south entrance (below left); Siegfried, Roy and a feline friend portrayed in bronze (below right)

Secret Garden Next to the Dolphin Habitat, Siegfried and Roy's Secret Garden re-creates a comfortable jungle haven for five rare breeds of big cats: white lions of Timbavati, heterozygous Bengal tigers (possessing both tawny and white genes), the royal white tigers of Nevada, a panther and a snow leopard. The Secret Garden's newest additions arrived in June 2008—white, white-striped and golden tiger cubs. When there are cubs in the Garden a special nursery area is created for them and they are just adorable to watch.

Siegfried and Roy Illusionists Siegfried and Roy and their majestic tigers have enthralled crowds with their stage show at the Mirage since 1989. Unfortunately the performers' show was suspended in 2003 after Roy was mauled by one of their cats.

THE BASICS

www.miragehabitat.com
✚ C8
✉ The Mirage, 3400 Las Vegas Boulevard South
☎ 702/791-7188
🕐 Mon–Fri 11–5.30, Sat, Sun 10–5.30 (longer hours in summer); last admission 30 min before closing
🍴 Several cafés and restaurants at the Mirage
🚌 Deuce
♿ Moderate

Imperial Palace Auto Collections

Dazzling examples at one of the largest automobile showrooms in the world

THE BASICS

www.autocollections.com

D8–D9

Imperial Palace, 3535 Las Vegas Boulevard South

702/794-3174

Daily 9.30–9.30

Several cafés and restaurants at the Imperial Palace

Harrah's/Imperial Palace

Deuce

Inexpensive

Gift shop

DID YOU KNOW?

● Because of his germ phobia, Howard Hughes installed an air-purification system into his 1954 Chrysler that cost more than the car.

● President Truman's 1950 Lincoln Cosmopolitan had a gold-plated interior.

● The 1933 Silver Arrow displayed at the museum is one of only three still in existence today.

The fifth level of the Imperial Palace parking facility takes on a rather different look from the other floors—this luxurious space displays a stunning collection of classic and special-interest cars, spanning a century of motoring.

Plush parking You could easily spend hours here, in what is one of the finest and largest automobile showrooms in the world. When it opened in 1981 the collection had 200 vehicles; since then, this number has increased to an impressive 750, although only around 250 are displayed at one time. There are gleaming examples of all those classics that generations of drivers have yearned for, there are rare and exclusive models, and there are cars that represent landmarks in vehicle construction and technology. A significant acquisition for the exhibition here is the world's largest collection of Model J. Duesenbergs.

Famous and infamous owners Some of the vehicles that hold the greatest fascination are those that are noteworthy because of the people who drove them. You might see Marilyn Monroe's pink 1955 Lincoln Capri convertible, an armor-plated 1939 Mercedes-Benz used by Adolph Hitler, and cars owned by Al Capone, Elvis Presley, Benito Mussolini and James Cagney. There's no certainty about what will be on show because this is not exactly a straightforward museum, and the collection is not necessarily a permanent one. All of the exhibits are for sale, and serious buyers may well be among your fellow browsers on the lot.

Enter the gateway to the stars and hang out with the celebs—even if they are made of wax

It is fitting that Madame Tussaud's first foray into the United States should be in Las Vegas, a magnet for both the biggest showbiz personalities and the most ardent celebrity-spotters.

Making an impression Madame Tussaud's is the world leader when it comes to making realistic likenesses in wax of the rich, famous and infamous. The secret is that they take an impression from the real person, rather than simply use an artist's sculpture, so every detail is absolutely spot on. Though this can be a rather claustrophobic experience (Napoleon was famously freaked out by it), celebrities regard it as at least one of the signs that they have made it in the business.

Las Vegas legends Not surprisingly, pride of place here goes to the superstars who have made their mark in Vegas—Wayne Newton, Elvis Presley, Engelbert Humperdinck, Tom Jones and the Rat Pack, to name just a few. Among more than 100 other masterfully produced figures is an international cast of movie and TV stars, icons from the music world and sport's big achievers.

Interactive experience Some exhibits allow you to interact with the famous models by taking part in a scenario, such as auditioning in front of Simon Cowell for American Idol. The highlight for every woman must be the "Marry Clooney" exhibit, where you put on a wedding gown and walk down the aisle with the gorgeous George himself—in your dreams!

THE BASICS

www.mtvegas.com
⊞ D8
✉ The Venetian, 3377 Las Vegas Boulevard South
☎ 702/862-7800
🕐 Daily 10–10 (closing times vary seasonally)
🍴 Several cafés and restaurants at the Venetian
🚌 Deuce
✋ Expensive

HIGHLIGHTS

● "The King in Concert"
● "Marry Clooney"
● SCREAM–the Chamber of Horrors

The Mirage

- Volcanic eruption
- Secret Garden and white tigers
- Dolphin Habitat

- Note that the volcano eruption will be cancelled during bad weather or high winds.

There is nothing so fascinating as the power of nature, and to watch the Mirage's simulated volcano erupt or come face-to-face with the magnificent wildlife is a highlight that will enhance anyone's day.

Tropical delights This Polynesian-style resort is fronted by cascading waterfalls, tropical foliage and an imitation volcano. As you enter the lobby you can't miss the huge coral-reef aquarium stocked with tropical fish. Venture farther in and you will discover a lush rain forest under a large atrium.

Eruptions to order You can wait years for a real volcano to create its spectacle, but here, in front of the Mirage, you can set your watch by it. The newly renovated spectacular two-minute show

Where there's smoke there's fire, and these are real flames erupting from the Mirage's volcano (left); one of the hotel's chic dining rooms (below left); the Mirage in neons (below right); a lush rain forest in the hotel atrium (below center)

starts with a rumbling sound, then a fog swirls around and a column of smoke and fire shoots more than 12ft (3.5m) into the sky. The show includes the latest special effects, with real flames on the water of the lagoon and state-of-the-art lighting techniques and sound systems. Arrive in good time to stake out a front-row position.

Other attractions The Mirage is also home to Siegfried and Roy's Secret Garden and Dolphin Habitat (▷ 48–49). The habitats serve as educational centers for guests and school children in the community. Since opening in 1997, the Secret Garden has endeavored to renew the public's sense of responsibility to preserve nature. The Cirque du Soleil creation LOVE (▷ 59) is presented at the Mirage and celebrates the musical legacy of The Beatles.

THE BASICS

www.themirage.com

✚ C8–D8

✉ 3400 Las Vegas Boulevard South

☎ 702/791-7111

🕐 Volcanic eruption: dusk–midnight on the hour

🍴 Several cafés and restaurants

🚌 Deuce

👤 Volcanic eruption: free

Paris Las Vegas

A taste of chic Paris, with fountain-splashed squares and grand facade of the Eiffel Tower

THE BASICS

www.parislasvegas.com
🔶 D9
✉ 3655 Las Vegas
Boulevard South
☎ 702/946-7000
🕐 Eiffel Tower Experience:
daily 10am–1am (weather
permitting)
🍴 Several cafés and
restaurants
🚊 Bally's/Paris
🚌 Deuce
♿ Eiffel Tower Experience:
moderate

HIGHLIGHTS

● Views from the Eiffel
Tower Observation Deck
● Shopping at Le Boulevard

Striving to capture the Parisian style of the most elegant of European cities, this hotel has succeeded in creating fine likenesses of the Eiffel Tower, Arc de Triomphe, Paris Opera House and the Louvre.

Joie de vivre This eye-catching resort may not be the real thing, but a characteristic exuberance is reflected in little touches like singing breadmen on bikes dressed in striped shirts and berets, and a joyful "Bonjour!" from roving street performers.

Eiffel Tower Experience The symbol of this hotel is the 525ft (160m) Eiffel Tower (half the size of the original), which was re-created using Gustav Eiffel's blueprints. A glass elevator takes you to the observation deck on the 50th floor for spectacular views of Las Vegas and the surrounding mountains—especially impressive at dusk when the Strip lights up. Eleven floors above the Strip is the sophisticated and pricey Eiffel Tower restaurant and bar.

Le Boulevard Don't miss this French-style shopping boulevard, which gives you a taste of one of Europe's most lively cities. The 31,000sq ft (2,880sq m) of retail space connects Paris Las Vegas to Bally's, the resort's sister property. Amid winding alleyways and cobbled streets, the ornate facades conceal elegant French boutiques, shops and restaurants. Weathered brickwork and brass lamps give an authentic rustic finish, and window boxes overflowing with bright blooms complete the Parisian picture.

The glamorous Planet Hollywood (left); Fashion at Miracle Mile (right)

Planet Hollywood and Miracle Mile

Out goes the Middle Eastern theme and in comes a more streamlined, urbanized feel—Planet Hollywood has made its transition from the former Aladdin hotel to the bright streets of glitzy Hollywood.

Just like Times Square Massive LED signs with continually flashing images certainly spark up this part of the Strip, and step inside the Planet to find an even more dramatic scene of highly polished black-granite floors and a color-shifting backdrop.

Shopping with a difference Make no mistake Miracle Mile is a shopping mall, with over 170 popular international retailers, many eateries and a plethora of entertainment venues, but it couldn't be farther from just an ordinary retail experience. Although mostly very snazzy with a silver grid ceiling, the transformation is ongoing and in places its former Moroccan roots are still evident. Check out the latest performances that take place at the V Theater (▷ 65). Shoppers can pause to view the multi-sensory laser show that plays hourly at the south entrance.

Stormy weather Miracle Mile is home to the bustling Merchant's Harbor, complete with the sounds of lapping waves and deckhands rushing back and forth from the freighter moored on the dockside. At regular intervals you will hear the rumble of distant thunder as a storm begins to brew. Clouds gather and gentle rain falls on the harbor, although you won't need an umbrella from your viewpoint on the shore.

THE BASICS

www.planetholly woodresort.com

🔢 D9

✉ 3667 Las Vegas Boulevard South

☎ 702/785-5555

🕐 Miracle Mile Sun–Thu 10–11, Fri–Sat 10–midnight; rainstorm every hour Mon–Thu, Fri–Sun every half hour

🍴 Several cafés and restaurants

🚌 Bally's/Paris

🚌 Deuce

HIGHLIGHTS

● The rainstorm outside Merchant's Harbor Coffee House

● Gregory Popvich's Comedy Pet Theater Show

The Venetian

HIGHLIGHTS

● St. Mark's Square
● Grand Canal
● Street entertainers
● Grand Canal Shoppes
● Madame Tussaud's
Celebrity Encounter

TIPS

● Reservations for gondola
rides must be made in
person on the same day.
● You will have to walk a lot
to see the whole complex;
wear comfortable shoes.

**Owner Sheldon Adelson's replica of
Venice has gone a long way to catch the
flavour of this most romantic city. But at
the same time it has retained all the glitz
and pizzazz expected from Las Vegas.**

Most authentic This $1.5 billion resort is one
of the city's most aesthetically pleasing properties.
The ornate lobby has domed and vaulted ceilings,
exquisite marble floors and reproductions of
frescoes framed in gold. An excellent take on
Venice, it has its own 1,200ft-long (365m) Grand
Canal—the real one extends 2.5 miles (4km).
The waterway meanders under arched bridges,
including the Rialto, and past the vibrant piazza of
St. Mark's Square where living statues amaze visitors
with their immovable poses. In the casino hang the
replica works of artists Tiepolo, Tintoretto and Titian.

The stunning opulence of the Venetian's lobby (left); masterpieces adorn the casino ceiling (right); the Grand Canal (below left) and St. Mark's campanile (top middle) re-created on the Strip; get in the swim of things at the pool complex (below middle); a singing gondolier takes guests on a musical journey (below right)

The Venetian is also home to Madame Tussaud's interactive wax museum (▷ 51).

Gondola ride From St. Mark's you can board a gondola and be carried down the Grand Canal to the soothing sound of water lapping against the sides; there is even a wedding gondola if you want to take the plunge. Everything looks particularly spectacular at dusk, when the spirit of Venice is really captured.

Time to shop The Grand Canal Shoppes mall lines an indoor cobblestoned plaza alongside the canal and is linked by walkways. There are fine restaurants and interesting shops behind faux facades where strolling opera singers perform Italian arias and various other street entertainers do their thing.

THE BASICS

www.venetian.com

✚ D8

✉ 3355 Las Vegas Boulevard South

☎ 702/414-1000. Grand Canal Shoppes/gondola ride: 702/414-4500

⏰ Gondola ride: Sun–Thu 10am–11pm, Fri, Sat 10am–midnight; last ride leaves 15 min before closing

🍴 Several cafés and restaurants

🚌 Deuce

♿ Gondola ride: moderate

More to See

ATOMIC TESTING MUSEUM

www.atomictestingmuseum.org

Opened in February 2005, this is the first museum of its kind in the US and provides an interesting insight into the work of the Nevada Test Site and its impact. Three miles (5km) from the Strip, the museum is certainly something different and a long way from the superficial hype of Vegas. Interactive exhibits help you learn about the history of nuclear power.

🚼 F9 ✉ 755 East Flamingo Road ☎ 702/794-5151 🕐 Mon–Sat 9–5, Sun 1–5 🚌 202 👋 Moderate

THE BEATLES LOVE

www.themirage.com

Another Cirque du Soleil production, LOVE celebrates the musical legacy of The Beatles and explores their songs in a series of scenes inhabited by real and imaginary people. Staged in a purpose-built circular theater.

🚼 D8 ✉ The Mirage, 3400 Las Vegas Boulevard South ☎ 702/792-7777 🕐 Thu–Mon 7pm and 10pm 🚌 Deuce 👋 Very Expensive

BELLAGIO GALLERY OF FINE ART

www.bellagiolasvegas.com

The first gallery on the Strip, showing a serious side to Las Vegas culture. The facility is a non-commercial venue that showcases two high-quality art exhibitions per year from major museums across the US and beyond.

🚼 D9 ✉ Bellagio, 3600 Las Vegas Boulevard South ☎ 702/693-7111 🕐 Sun–Thu 10–6, Fri–Sat 10–9; last admission 30 mins before 🚌 Deuce 👋 Moderate

BLUE MAN GROUP

www.venetian.com

The most unusual show in Vegas—a group of guys with bright cobalt-blue bald heads, performing hilarious routines in which artistic canvases are created by the strangest means.

🚼 D8 ✉ The Venetian, 3355 Las Vegas Boulevard South ☎ 702/414-1000 🕐 7pm and 10pm 🚌 Deuce 👋 Very expensive

CITYCENTER

www.citycenter.com

This towering urban metropolis has

The weird and wonderful Blue Man Group

created an unparalleled skyline that defines a changing Las Vegas skyline. The work of eight different architects, the city within a city centers round the ARIA gaming resort, which houses the latest Cirque du Soleil show—a tribute to Elvis. Three non-gaming luxury hotels, residential condominiums and a sparkling retail and entertainment district, Crystals, join ARIA. A feature is the $40 million public art program, which showcases many acclaimed artists. All of this has been created with a commitment to the conservation of water, energy and air quality.

🕂 D9 ✉ Las Vegas Boulevard South (between Bellagio and Harmon Avenue) ☎ 702/590-7171 🚌 Duece

FLAMINGO WILDLIFE HABITAT
www.flamingolasvegas.com
A lush 15-acre (6ha) paradise has been re-created at the Flamingo to provide a home to more than 300 exotic birds, including flamingos and penguins.

🕂 D9 ✉ Flamingo, 3555 Las Vegas

Boulevard South ☎ 702/733-3111 🕐 Daily 24 hours 🚇 Flamingo/Caesars 🚌 Deuce 💵 Free

JUBILEE!
www.ballyslasvegas.com
Jubilee's scantily clad showgirls in massive headdresses and little else—many appear topless—remain as popular as when the show opened in 1981. Though the original concept remains unchanged, brand-new routines and segments are introduced on a regular basis.

🕂 D9 ✉ Bally's, 3645 Las Vegas Boulevard South ☎ 702/967 4567 🕐 Sat–Thu 7.30pm and 10.30pm 🚇 Bally's/Paris 🚌 Deuce 💵 Very expensive ❓ Minimum age limit 18 years

PENN AND TELLER
www.riolasvegas.com
This talented partnership combines magic, illusions, juggling, comedy and stunts in an intelligent show.

🕂 B8 ✉ Rio, 3700 West Flamingo Road ☎ 702/777-7776 🕐 Daily 9pm 🚌 202 💵 Very expensive

Bring on the dancing girls, Jubilee!

An oasis of calm at the Flamingo

PHANTOM OF THE OPERA

www.phantomlasvegas.com

Andrew Lloyd Webber's musical phenomenon opened in 2006 in the majestic grandeur of the Venetian.

🔺 D8 ✉ The Venetian, 3355 Las Vegas Boulevard South ☎ 702/414-9000 🕐 Mon–Sat 7pm (also 9.30pm Tue, Sat) 🚌 Deuce 💵 Very expensive

SHOW IN THE SKY

www.riolasvegas.com

It's carnival time every day at the Rio. Mardi Gras floats suspended from the ceiling parade above the casino floor and for a fee you can take a magical ride on board.

🔺 B8 ✉ Rio, 3700 West Flamingo Road ☎ 702/777-7777 🕐 Shows Thu–Sun hourly 7pm–midnight 🚌 202 💵 Show free; ride moderate

SIRENS OF TI

www.treasureisland.com

A swashbuckling battle between sexy sirens and renegade pirates that takes place at Siren's Cove, at the hotel entrance. There's music, seductive dancing and plenty of loud explosions.

🔺 D8 ✉ Treasure Island, 3300 Las Vegas Boulevard South ☎ 702/894-7111 🕐 Nightly 5.30, 7, 8.30, 10 (dependent on weather); shows last 90 min 🚌 Deuce 💵 Free

TONY N' TINA'S WEDDING

www.tonyandtinavegas.com

Considered one of the best and most successful Off-Broadway shows Tony n' Tina's Wedding arrived at Planet Hollywood in 2002. This is a show with a difference. If you don't get to go to a real wedding while you are in Vegas come here for the next best thing. Audience participation is key and everyone gets to attend the wildest and most raucous Italian-American ceremony and reception. You even get the Italian buffet, complete with wedding cake.

🔺 D9 ✉ Planet Hollywood Resort, 3367 Las Vegas Boulevard South ☎ 702/785-5555 (702/949-6450 for tickets) 🕐 Mon–Sat 7pm 🚌 Bally's/Paris 🚌 Deuce; Strip trolley 💵 Expensive

Let battle commence, Sirens of TI

Heart of the Strip

A walk through the heart of the Strip, stopping at some of the major resort hotels to experience a sample of what they have to offer.

DISTANCE: About 2 miles (3km) **ALLOW:** 3 hours

START

MIRACLE MILE
🔶 D9 🚌 Deuce

END

THE VENETIAN
🔶 D8 🚌 Deuce

❶ Wander through the sparkling new Miracle Mile shopping mall (▷ 55). Stick around long enough to do a spot of window shopping and admire the sleek surroundings.

❽ Choose one of the many refreshment stops to recharge your batteries and then take a relaxing gondola ride to finish your walk.

❷ Back outside, walk north to Paris (▷ 54) and take the elevator to the top of the Eiffel Tower. Go north to Ballys and cross the bridge over the boulevard to Bellagio (▷ 46), home to the ultimate water attraction.

❼ Cross the footbridge over to the Venetian (▷ 56), where the cityscape of Venice has been replicated. Here you'll find a network of canals, lined by Venetian-style architecture and crossed by pretty little bridges where you can while away the time.

❸ From inside Bellagio, take the elevated walkway across Flamingo Road to Caesars Palace (▷ 47) for the Atlantis talking statue show.

❻ From the Mirage, walk north on the Strip until you get to the Treasure Island resort (if operating, hop on the tram if you want to take the strain off your feet). Try to time it right for the start of the Sirens of TI show (▷ 61).

❹ Go left from Caesars Palace to the Mirage (▷ 52). Out the back you can watch the dolphins play for a while and then move on to see the big cats that live here.

❺ Retrace your steps back through the hotel. Note the aquarium in reception.

WALK

CENTRAL STRIP

Shopping

ALEXANDER KALIFANO
www.kalifano.com
Inside Bally's Monorail Mall, Alexander Kalifano displays the finest gemstone globes at discount prices, handmade by the Kalifano family for over four generations.
➕ D9 ⊠ Bally's, 3645 Las Vegas Boulevard South
☎ 702/791-5501
🚍 Bally's/Paris 🚍 Deuce

ALPACA PETE'S
www.alpacapetes.com
Quality alpaca yarn products handcrafted from all over the world using the finest materials. Rugs are the signature product but you will find products such as slippers, sweaters and soft furnishings.
➕ D8 ⊠ Miracle Mile, 3663 Las Vegas Boulevard South
☎ 702/862-8297
🚍 Bally's/Paris 🚍 Deuce

BARNES & NOBLE
This is one of several Vegas branches of the colossally well stocked general bookstore. It has impressive children's and best-seller sections.
➕ G7 ⊠ 3860 South Maryland Parkway
☎ 702/734-2900 🚍 109

CAROLINA HERRERA
This store is dedicated to Herrera's lifestyle collection for men and women. The range includes chic tailored suits, glam evening wear, cotton shirts and accessories.
➕ D8 ⊠ The Forum, 3570 Las Vegas Boulevard South
☎ 702/894-5242 🚍 Deuce

CHIHULY STORE
This shop has a good representation of the respected glass sculptor's vibrant hand-blown pieces. It is fitting that Chihuly opened his first gallery here—his biggest sculpture hangs from the Bellagio's lobby ceiling (▷ 46).
➕ D9 ⊠ Via Fiore Bellagio, 3600 Las Vegas Boulevard South ☎ 702/693-7995
🚍 Deuce

FIELD OF DREAMS
This is the place for one-off sport and celebrity memorabilia

---

---

such as an electric guitar signed by musician Carlos Santana to a jersey autographed by football player Dan Marino.
➕ B8 ⊠ Masquerade Village, Rio, 3700 West Flamingo Road ☎ 702/777-7777 🚍 202

GIANNI VERSACE
The late designer's Italian style is obvious in the garments sold here, all made from the finest fabrics. The company's signature lion's head appears on everything.
➕ D8 ⊠ The Forum, 3570 Las Vegas Boulevard South
☎ 702/796-7222 🚍 Deuce

GRAND CANAL SHOPPES
This chic Italian-theme mall stretches along a replica of Venice's Grand Canal. Here you'll find over 80 of the most exclusive stores in the world, ranging from Davidoff cigars to designer shoes.
➕ D8 ⊠ The Venetian, 3355 Las Vegas Boulevard South
☎ 702/414-1000 🚍 Deuce

MASQUERADE VILLAGE
Stroll down the tiled streets here to find quirky places such as the Nawlins Store, carrying voodoo supplies and good luck charms. Elsewhere in the mall, sportswear and memorabilia are on sale.
➕ B8 ⊠ Rio, 3700 West Flamingo Road ☎ 702/777-7777 🚍 202

MIKIMOTO

Exquisite Akoya cultured pearls and South Sea pearl jewelry are sold here among other gift items.

➕ D8 ✉ Grand Canal Shoppes, 3355 Las Vegas Boulevard South ☎ 702/414-3900 🚌 Deuce

SHOPPES AT THE PALAZZO

www.theshoppesatthe palazzo.com
Stylish shopping awaits at the Palazzo, anchored by Barneys New York, as well as more than 60 international boutiques, including Christian Louboutin and Jimmy Choo.

➕ D8 ✉ The Palazzo, 3325 Las Vegas Boulevard South ☎ 702/607-7777 🚌 Deuce

SHOWCASE SLOTS & ANTIQUES

A nostalgic collection of antique slot machines, early video poker machines, jukeboxes and neon signs.

➕ D6 ✉ Miracle Mile, 3663 Las Vegas Boulevard South ☎ 702/740-5722 🚌 Deuce

VIA BELLAGIO

This opulent mall has exquisite fashion and jewelry collections from world-renowned designers Chanel, Gucci, Prada, Tiffany & Co. and lots more.

➕ C9 ✉ Bellagio, 3600 Las Vegas Boulevard South ☎ 702/693-7111 🚌 Deuce

Entertainment and Nightlife

CLEOPATRA'S BARGE

www.caesarspalace.com
This floating club is a replica of the vessel that carried the Egyptian Queen Cleopatra along the Nile. During the week, a DJ plays contemporary dance music, and there's live music on weekends.

➕ D8 ✉ Caesars Palace, 3570 Las Vegas Boulevard South ☎ 702/731-7110 🚌 Deuce

COLOSSEUM

www.caesarspalace.com
A magnificent auditorium purpose-built to stage exciting extravaganzas featuring international superstars.

➕ D8 ✉ Caesars Palace, 3570 Las Vegas Boulevard South ☎ 702/731-7110 🚍 Flamingo/Caesars 🚌 Deuce

FLAMINGO SHOWROOM

www.flamingolasvegas.com
From the very beginning the Flamingo has hosted show business legends—Nat King Cole and Jerry Lewis have graced the stage here. Currently, singer Toni Braxton is appearing, plus top comedy group Second City.

➕ D9 ✉ Flamingo, 3555 Las Vegas Boulevard South ☎ 702/733-3111 🚍 Flamingo/Caesars 🚌 Deuce

GHOSTBAR

www.palms.com
One of Vegas's most talked about bars, with a simple, yet eclectic look, is atop the Palms Hotel. Marvel at the breathtaking views from 55 floors up while music from the DJ fills the background. From the outside deck is yet another fantastic view, one from a glass floor looking directly down at the Palms Pool below. A young and trendy crowd mix with the celebrity clientele.

➕ A9 ✉ Palms, 4321 Flamingo Road ☎ 702/942-6832 🚌 202

GORDON-BIERSCH LAS VEGAS

www.gordonbiersch.com
Exposed pipes and gleaming brewing equipment set the stage for this hangout, popular with local yuppies. The beers include tasty German brews that are changed seasonally.

➕ F7 ✉ 3987 Paradise Road ☎ 702/312-5247 🚌 108

IMPROV COMEDY CLUB

www.harrahs.com

Four comedy shows a night (except Mon) feature emerging stars from a branch of the famous Improv comedy club.

🔼 D8 ✉ Harrah's, 3475 Las Vegas Boulevard South ☎ 702/702-369 🚇 Harrah's/ Imperial Palace 🚌 Deuce

JAPONAIS

www.themirage.com

Relax in this exotic lounge amid tropical foliage and lulled by the soothing sound of waterfalls.

🔼 D8 ✉ The Mirage, 3400 Las Vegas Boulevard South ☎ 702/792-7979 🚌 Deuce

MIST BAR

www.treasureisland.com

A lively crowd comes to this relaxed spot, with its neighborhood-bar atmosphere, to watch sports on large plasma screens and to listen to rock and pop.

🔼 D8 ✉ Treasure Island, 3300 Las Vegas Boulevard South ☎ 702/894-7111 🚌 Deuce

NAPOLEON'S

www.parislasvegas.com

The French theme at this champagne bar incorporates over 100 varieties of the world's finest, and French-style hot and cold appetizers. Live jazz until the early hours.

🔼 D9 ✉ Paris Las Vegas, 3655 Las Vegas Boulevard South ☎ 702/946-7000 🚇 Bally's/Paris 🚌 Deuce

PRIVÉ

www.privelv.com

From the high-end service, dance floor made from Brazilian cherry and entrance arch adorned with illuminated crystal garlands, Privé at the Planet attracts just as many celebrities as it has in Miami over the years.

🔼 D8 ✉ Planet Hollywood, 3667 Las Vegas Boulevard South ☎ 702/523-6002 🚌 Bally's/Paris 🚌 Deuce

RISQUÉ

www.parislasvegas.com

A sensual ultralounge attracting a sophisticated crowd with velvet drapes, crystal chandeliers, mirrored lighting effects and a lit dance floor where music plays well into the night. Intimate balconies offer views over the Strip.

CIRQUE DU SOLEIL

This troupe, originally from Quebec in Canada, has taken circus arts to new levels with its breathtaking skills and supremely artistic concept shows. It has won over Las Vegas, with several shows currently running: **Mystère** at Treasure Island (Sat–Wed); **"O"** at Bellagio (Wed–Sun); **Zumanity** at New York-New York (Fri–Wed); **Kà** at MGM Grand (Tue–Sat); **The Beatles Love** at the Mirage (▷ 59); **Criss Angel: Believe** at Luxor. For further details, www.cirquedusoleil.com

🔼 D9 ✉ Paris Las Vegas, 3655 Las Vegas Boulevard South ☎ 702/946-7000 🚇 Bally's/Paris 🚌 Deuce

UNLV PERFORMING ARTS CENTER

http://.pac.unlv.edu

See major international artists perform classical and popular music, dance, theater, ballet and opera. The center comprises the Artemus W. Ham Concert Hall (home to the Nevada Symphony Orchestra), the Judy Bayley Theater and the Black Box Theater.

🔼 G9 ✉ University of Nevada, 4505 South Maryland Parkway ☎ 702/895-3535 🚌 109

V BAR

www.venetian.com

Enclosed in opaque glass walls, this high-roller's joint oozes sophistication. Sleek lines, leather chaise longues and subdued lighting enhance the sultry atmosphere.

🔼 D8 ✉ The Venetian, 3355 Las Vegas Boulevard South ☎ 702/414-1000 🚌 Deuce

V THEATER

www.varietytheater.com

A specially tailored venue that showcases a varied program during the day and evening, ranging from comedy, variety and magic to game shows and tribute acts.

🔼 D8 ✉ Miracle Mile, 3663 Las Vegas Boulevard South ☎ 702/892-7792 🚌 Bally's/Paris 🚌 Deuce

Restaurants

BATTISTA'S HOLE IN THE WALL ($$)

www.battistaslasvegas.com
For more than 30 years
people have been flocking here for the excellent
Italian food, served
with style.
🚩 D9 ⊠ 4041 Audrie Street
☎ 702/732-1424 🕐 Daily
5–10.30 🚌 Flamingo/Caesars
🚌 Deuce

BELLAGIO BUFFET ($$)

More expensive than
most buffets, this is
probably the most highly
regarded. It has many
different types of cuisine,
including Italian, Chinese
and Japanese, in a
European marketplace-
style setting.
🚩 C9 ⊠ Bellagio, 3600 Las
Vegas Boulevard South
☎ 702/693-7111 🕐 Daily
7am–10pm 🚌 Deuce

BOUCHON ($$)

www.bouchonbistro.com
World-renowned chef
Thomas Keller showcases his bistro fare,
delighting both the
palate and the eye, at
Bouchon, located in the
Venetian Tower. Deep
blue velvet seating,
antique lights, a mosaic

floor and hand-painted
murals provide a sophisticated café-style ambience
amid an enchanting pool-
side garden.
🚩 D8 ⊠ The Venetian 3355
Las Vegas Boulevard South
☎ 702/414-6200 🕐 Daily
7–10.30, 5–10.30, also Sat, Sun
8–2 🚌 Deuce

BRADLEY OGDEN ($$$)

www.caesarspalace.com
This famed San Francisco
chef has earned national
acclaim for his classic,
fresh American cooking.
Polished floors and dark
wood give a sleek look to
the elegant and refined
dining room where
serious, quality food is
served by first-class
professional staff.
🚩 D8 ⊠ Caesars Palace,
3750 Las Vegas Boulevard
South ☎ 702/731-7110

BUFFET KNOW-HOW

Buffets offer breakfast, lunch
and dinner, with a different
range of food available at
each meal. They are a great
option for families, particularly those that include fussy
eaters, because there is sure
to be something for everyone. Buffets also offer
tremendous value for the
money. This does, of course,
mean that they are popular
and lines can be long, especially at peak times—at the
most popular buffets, you
may need to allow up to
three hours for your meal.

🕐 Wed–Sun 5–11
🚌 Flamingo/Caesars
🚌 Deuce

CANALETTO ($$$)

www.venetian.com
Where better to sample
good northern Italian
cuisine than on a re-
creation of Venice's
St. Mark's Square? Some
little-known Italian wines
are on offer, too.
🚩 D8 ⊠ The Venetian, 3355
Las Vegas Boulevard South
☎ 702/733-0122
🕐 Sun–Thu 11.30–11, Fri, Sat
11.30–midnight 🚌 Deuce

CARNIVAL WORLD ($$)

www.riolasvegas.com
This is one of the best
buffets in Las Vegas, with
chefs cooking on view at
various points around the
serving islands. There are
11 styles of cuisine, from
Brazilian to Mongolian.
🚩 B8 ⊠ Rio, 3700 West
Flamingo Road ☎ 702/777-
7777 🕐 Mon–Fri 7–10, Sat,
Sun 7.30–10 🚌 202

DOS CAMINOS ($$–$$$)

www.brguestrestaurants.com
Dos Caminos delights
with its authentic,
innovative fare such as
classic staples; empanada
and frijoles borrachos
("drunken beans").
They serve a mean
cochinita pibil (slow-roast-
ed pig), so tender it falls
apart at a touch of the
fork. The surroundings
are equally inventive:
shimmering copper glass

and gold and fuchsia tiles on the wall.
🔲 D8 ✉ Palazzo, 3325 Las Vegas Boulevard South ☎ 702/577-9600 🕐 Daily 11–11 🚌 Deuce

FRANCESCO'S ($$)
www.treasureisland.com
Superb Neapolitan pizza and pastas at this friendly restaurant. Good house wines by the carafe.
🔲 D8 ✉ Treasure Island, 3300 Las Vegas Boulevard South ☎ 702/894-7111 🕐 Wed, Thu, Sun 5–11, Fri–Sat until midnight 🚌 Deuce

HARLEY DAVIDSON CAFÉ ($)
www.harley-davidsoncafe.com
Motorcycle buffs will enthuse over this American roadside café. Many gleaming machines are on display, including one owned by Elvis, and memorabilia covers the walls. Try the tollhouse-cookie pie.
🔲 D9 ✉ 3725 Las Vegas Boulevard South ☎ 702/740-4555 🕐 Sun–Thu 11–11, Fri, Sat 11am–midnight 🚌 Deuce

HOUSE OF LORDS ($$)
www.saharavegas.com
Once the haunt of visiting stars, this comfortable restaurant remains popular for its traditional cuisine. Dishes include roasted crab cakes, prime rib and cherries jubilee.
🔲 F6 ✉ Sahara, 2535 Las Vegas Boulevard South ☎ 702/737-2111

🕐 Mon–Thu 5–10, Fri, Sat 5–11 🚇 Sahara 🚌 Deuce

HYAKUMI ($$)
www.caesarspalace.com
This is another Japanese restaurant where teppan-yaki chefs prepare your meal at your table with great flair and entertainment value. There's a good range of sake, too.
🔲 D8 ✉ Caesars Palace, 3570 Las Vegas Boulevard South ☎ 702/731-7110 🕐 Daily 11–3, 5–11 🚇 Flamingo/Caesars 🚌 Deuce

KOI ($$$)
www.koirestaurant.com
This Vegas outpost of the New York hotspot exudes a sophisticated tone. Koi

---

TASTE THE GOOD LIFE

In addition to the endless variety of eateries catering to visitors on a more restricted budget, a new type of restaurant has surfaced in Las Vegas. During the 1990s, fashionable eateries and stand-alone fine-dining establishments made their mark on the city. World-famous chefs with the best credentials—such as Puck, Lagasse, Palmer, Vongerichten, Mori, Sotelino and Matsuisa—were lured to Vegas to meet the demands of increasing numbers of sophisticated travelers visiting the city. As a result, food has evolved into another attraction with a Las Vegas flavor.

---

cooks up modern and traditional Japanese inspired dishes with a Californian accent; munch on Chilean sea bass and Kobe filet mignon, with one of the best views of the Bellagio fountains.
🔲 D8 ✉ Planet Hollywood, 3667 Las Vegas Boulevard South ☎ 702/454-4555 🕐 Sun–Thu 5.30–11, Fri–Sat 5.30–midnight 🚇 Bally's/Paris 🚌 Deuce

KOKOMO'S ($$)
www.themirage.com
Tropical surroundings complement the delicious Hawaiian cuisine, including fish with broiled bananas and coconut shrimp.
🔲 D8 ✉ The Mirage, 3400 Las Vegas Boulevard South ☎ 702/791-7111 🕐 Daily 5–10.30 🚌 Deuce

LAWRY'S THE PRIME RIB ($$$)
www.lawrysonline.com
Lawry's is popular for its perfectly cooked, tasty prime rib, which is carved at the table. Waitresses in stylish uniforms and starched white caps tend to your every need in the art deco surroundings.
🔲 E9 ✉ 4043 Howard Hughes Parkway ☎ 702/893-2223 🕐 Sun–Thu 5–10, Fri, Sat 5–11 🚌 202

MICHAEL MINA ($$$)
www.bellagiolasvegas.net
Enjoy seafood favorites that chef Michael Mina has made famous with his daring approach, using

unexpected flavors and textures blended with Mediterranean and Californian ingredients. Sleek, yet casual, this is the perfect place to try Mina's signature dishes.

🔢 C9 ✉ Bellagio, 3600 Las Vegas Boulevard South ☎ 702/693-7223 🕐 Daily 5–10 🚌 Deuce

MON AMI GABI ($$)
www.monamigabi.com
Enjoy fine French fare in the atrium (with an open sunroof) or on the patio. Tables are set beneath sparkling lights, from where you get a great view of the Bellagio's fountain show.

🔢 D9 ✉ Paris Las Vegas, 3655 Las Vegas Boulevard South 🕐 Sun–Thu 11.30–3, 4–11, Sat 11.30–3, 4–midnight 🚌 Bally's/Paris 🚌 Deuce

NERO'S ($$$)
www.caesarspalace.com
Maine lobster, swordfish and grilled ahi feature on the menu of this popular restaurant, along with hearty steaks.

🔢 D8 ✉ Caesars Palace, 3570 Las Vegas Boulevard South ☎ 702/731-7110 🕐 Daily 5–11 🚌 Flamingo/Caesars 🚌 Deuce

PAMPAS BRAZILIAN GRILLE ($$)
www.pampasusa.com
Come enjoy the true taste of Brazil. Sizzling skewers of the finest meats are bought to your

table in an endless parade while you feast on mountains of fresh produce and salads at the buffet.

🔢 D8 ✉ Miracle Mile, 3663 Las Vegas Boulevard South ☎ 702/737-4748 🕐 Daily 11.30–10 🚌 Bally's/Paris 🚌 Deuce

PARADISE GARDEN BUFFET ($$)
www.flamingolasvegas.com
Enjoy the view of cascading waterfalls and wildlife while you dine on crab, shrimp, prime rib, salads and everything else in between. There's also a large dessert choice.

🔢 D9 ✉ Flamingo, 3555 Las Vegas Boulevard ☎ 702/733-3333 🕐 Daily 7–3, 4–10 🚌 Flamingo/Caesars 🚌 Deuce

PICASSO ($$$)
www.bellagiolasvegas.com
This is among the best restaurants in Vegas, with refined cuisine reflecting places where the artist

---

JUST DESSERTS

If it's dessert you're after, then pay a visit to Lenôtre in Le Boulevard at Paris Las Vegas (▷ 52) for a mouth-watering assortment of French pastries, éclairs and cookies that can be enjoyed in a café-style atmosphere. At the Venetian (▷ 56–57), Tintoretto's Bakery also has luscious homemade pastries and cookies.

---

lived (south of France and Spain). The Picasso paintings on the walls are authentic.

🔢 C9 ✉ Bellagio, 3600 Las Vegas Boulevard South ☎ 702/693-7223 🕐 Wed–Mon 6–9.30 🚌 Deuce

POSTRIO ($$)
www.venetian.com
Enjoy celebrity chef Wolfgang Puck's American dishes in an elegant dining room or casual café on St. Mark's Square.

🔢 D8 ✉ The Venetian, 3355 Las Vegas Boulevard South ☎ 702/796-1110 🕐 Daily 11–4, 5.30–9 🚌 Deuce

VALENTINO ($$$)
www.venetian.com
Linger over superb modern Italian cuisine in a remarkable setting at this top-class restaurant, owned by unforgettable Piero Selvaggio.

🔢 D8 ✉ The Venetian, 3355 Las Vegas Boulevard South ☎ 702/414-3000 🕐 Daily 11.30–4, 4.30–11 🚌 Deuce

VILLAGE SEAFOOD ($$)
www.riolasvegas.com
Fish, fish and more fish—in fact, nothing but seafood is served here. Even so, there's plenty of choice, with dishes prepared in just about every way you could imagine.

🔢 B8 ✉ Rio, 3700 West Flamingo Road ☎ 702/777-7777 🕐 Sun–Thu 4–10, Fri–Sat 3.30–10.30 🚌 202

This stretch is a mixture of old and new. Steve Wynn's sparkling multimillion dollar hotel, Wynn Las Vegas, overshadows old faithfuls such as the Sahara and Circus Circus that were part of the Golden Era.

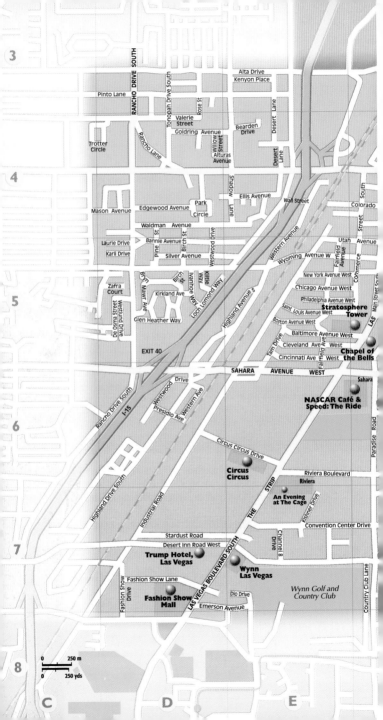

Circus Circus

HIGHLIGHTS

HIGHLIGHTS

- The Canyon Blaster ride
- The Rim Runner ride
- The Chaos ride
- FX Theater
- Big Top circus acts
- The Disk'o ride

TIPS

- Height restrictions may apply on some rides.
- If you're intending to stay a while at the Adventuredome, the daily pass can save you money.

The circus has come to town. In fact, it arrived here on the Strip in 1968, when Circus Circus opened its doors to provide the city with its first gaming concern offering family entertainment.

Roll up, roll up At first there were no hotel rooms at Circus Circus, only a casino and the world's biggest permanent circus tent. Today, however, around 1,500 guest rooms are stacked in towers behind the first-floor casino, while the upper floor has a wealth of carnival attractions and arcade games surrounding a circus arena. Acrobats, trapeze artists, aerialists and clowns are just some of the acts that perform daily under the big top.

Undercover thrills In 1993 the Adventuredome was added, said to be the biggest indoor theme

Try Adventuredome's thrilling rides, if you dare; Lucky the clown greets people at the big top (below left); bumper to bumper in the Adventuredome (below right)

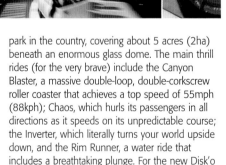

park in the country, covering about 5 acres (2ha) beneath an enormous glass dome. The main thrill rides (for the very brave) include the Canyon Blaster, a massive double-loop, double-corkscrew roller coaster that achieves a top speed of 55mph (88kph); Chaos, which hurls its passengers in all directions as it speeds on its unpredictable course; the Inverter, which literally turns your world upside down, and the Rim Runner, a water ride that includes a breathtaking plunge. For the new Disk'o ride you will need a strong stomach and for the 4-D experience check out the special FX Theater.

Gentler fun There are also less stressful activities, to please all ages. These include team laser tag and a climbing wall, while younger children will love the carousels, bumper cars and miniature golf.

THE BASICS

www.circuscircus.com

✚ E6

✉ 2880 Las Vegas Boulevard South

☎ 702/734-0410. Adventuredome: 702/ 794-3939

🕐 Midway Circus Acts: every half-hour 11am–midnight. Adventuredome: Mon–Thu 10–6, Fri, Sat 10am–midnight, Sun 10–9 (hours may vary seasonally)

🍴 Several cafés and restaurants

🚌 Deuce

♿ Adventuredome: free admission, charge for rides; daily pass expensive

NASCAR Café and Speed: The Ride

Speed (left) at the NASCAR Café bursts out into Sahara Avenue (right)

THE BASICS

www.saharavegas.com/NASCAR

🗺 F6

✉ Sahara, 2535 Las Vegas Boulevard South

☎ 702/734-7223

🕐 Cyber Speedway: Sun–Thu 10–midnight, Fri, Sat 10am–1am. Speed: Sun–Thu 11am–midnight, Fri, Sat 11am–1am

🚉 Sahara

🚌 Deuce

💲 Day pass: moderate

❓ You must be at least 54in (1.37m) tall to ride the Cyber Speedway

HIGHLIGHTS

● Meet the racing drivers when they are in town
● Cyber Speedway
● SPEED: The Ride

People are racing to this motor-sport theme café, with its state-of-the-art simulators, real stock cars, 3-D racing movies and the fastest roller coaster in the world winding in and out of the building.

NASCAR Café To call it a café hardly gives an accurate impression of this massive venue and its exciting attractions. But café it is, with 490 seats and an all-American menu. In addition, though, there are some amazing motor-racing exhibits, focusing on "Carzilla," the world's largest stock car. The upper level has eight regular-size stock cars suspended from the ceiling in racing formation, and there are about a dozen more cars around the place. While you munch on your lunch you can watch staff carry out a 20-second pitstop and see NASCAR news and driver profiles on giant screens. Would-be racing drivers can then try out their skills on the Las Vegas Cyber Speedway, where model stock cars are mounted on hydraulic bases with plenty of controls to personalize the ride.

Speed: The Ride Inside the café you can climb aboard this roller coaster, the fastest in the world, going from 0 to 40mph (64kph) in about two seconds, then accelerating to 70mph (113kph) as it bursts out of the building onto Sahara Avenue. The ride features a plunge through a tunnel, an exhilarating loop, a quick trip through the Sahara marquee and a stop at 224ft (68m) above ground…and then you cover the whole track again in reverse. This is not for the fainthearted, and is perhaps best experienced before you eat lunch!

Stratosphere Tower

If zooming up the tallest free-standing tower in the United States isn't exciting enough for you, the highest thrill rides in the world await you at the top, along with a revolving restaurant and breathtaking views.

On top of the world Marking the northern end of the Strip, the Stratosphere stands in the shadow of its 1,149ft (350m) tower, which is the main attraction. By means of speedy double-decker elevators, you can be at the 12-floor complex known as the pod, which starts at 833ft (254m), in less than 30 seconds and enjoy spectacular views from the indoor observation lounge or the open-air deck. Beneath this is the revolving Top of the World gourmet restaurant (▷ 82).

High-level thrills, low-level fun The attractions at the top of the tower are definitely not for anyone who suffers from vertigo. Big Shot, 921ft (281m) high, propels passengers upward at 45mph (72kph), creating a G-force of four, then plummets at zero gravity. X-Scream dangles you off the side of the building, shooting you out in a small car 27ft (8m) over the edge of the tower, some 866ft (264m) above the ground, 100 stories up, while Insanity is the ultimate in thrill rides—you experience centrifugal forces of three Gs while being spun out 64ft (19m) beyond the edge of the tower 900ft (274m) up. If you can't stand the pace or the height visit the Tower Shops, an international marketplace featuring themed streets reminiscent of Paris, New York and Hong Kong.

THE BASICS

www.stratospherehotel.com

🚩 F5

✉ 2000 Las Vegas Boulevard South

☎ 702/380-7777

🕐 Rides: Sun–Thu 10am–1am, Fri, Sat 10am–2am (hours vary seasonally)

🍴 Top of the World restaurant; coffee shop and four restaurants

🚌 Deuce

♿ Tower: moderate (no charge if you have a restaurant reservation). Individual rides, including admission to tower: moderate. Multiride ticket: expensive

❓ You must be at least 48in (1.22m) tall to ride the Big Shot, and 54in (1.38m) to ride X-Scream and Insanity

HIGHLIGHTS

● The view from the observation deck
● A gourmet meal in the Top of the World restaurant
● The thrill rides

Wedding Chapels

Whenever Cupid strikes, a Las Vegas chapel is a memorable place to tie the knot

THE BASICS

Graceland Chapel
✚ G4 ✉ 619 Las Vegas Boulevard South ☎ 702/382-0091; www.graceland chapel.com

Viva Las Vegas Wedding Chapel
✚ F4 ✉ 1205 Las Vegas Boulevard South
☎ 702/ 384-0771; www.vivalasvegas.com

Chapel of the Bells
✚ F5 ✉ 2233 Las Vegas Boulevard South ☎ 702/735-6803; www.chapelof thebellslasvegas.com

Little White Chapel
✚ F4 ✉ 1301 Las Vegas Boulevard South
☎ 702/382-5943; www.littlewhitechapel.com

HIGHLIGHTS

● Each chapel has a wedding planner for a stress-free ceremony.
● Whatever the happy couple visualize can become reality.
● Couples can get married any time of day.

Whether your ideal wedding is being married by Elvis, tying the knot in a hot-air balloon, going for the quick drive-through ceremony or just a traditional approach, Vegas will have a chapel that can oblige.

What your heart desires Many hotels have elegant wedding chapels, or you can opt for an outdoor location amid majestic Nevada mountains and canyons. Anything goes in Las Vegas. If you're going to the chapel and you're going to get married, then some of the chapels north of Sahara Avenue will provide a day to remember.

Gathered together in the sight of Elvis The Graceland Chapel and the Viva Las Vegas Wedding Chapel offer the most renowned style of wedding in Las Vegas, the ceremony that's conducted by an Elvis look-alike.

Chapel of the Bells Follow in the footsteps of Mickey Rooney, football legend Pelé and soldiers marrying before Desert Storm in this most polished of venues. Among their promotions are a free bottle of champagne and personalized wedding certificate.

Little White Chapel The setting of many celebrity weddings (including one of Joan Collins' marriages), with traditional ceremonies around the clock—simply show up and wait your turn. The Little White Chapel in the Sky marries couples in a hot-air balloon.

The Wynn Las Vegas is the epitomy of luxury, with grand architecture and designer stores

Wynn Las Vegas

This $2.7 billion resort opened in 2005, a stunning creation by Las Vegas entrepreneur and developer Steve Wynn. If you can't afford to stay here, there's nothing to stop you gazing at its magnificence.

Dazzling splendor This incredible showpiece covers 215 acres (87ha) and is one of the tallest buildings in Vegas, towering 60 stories over the Strip. The grounds are an evergreen oasis with trickling streams, the scent of fresh flowers and an integrated 18-hole golf course (open to guests only).

Spectacles for free A lagoon backed by a 150ft (46m) man-made mountain, complete with waterfall, takes center stage. A visual spectacular, the Lake of Dreams, is projected onto the water and a screen that rises out of the lagoon. Window-shop on Wynn Esplanade (▷ 80), with its collection of designer shops, and visit the full-size Ferrari-Maserati dealership, where some of the most yearned after cars in the world are displayed. Steve Wynn's personal art collection is scattered throughout the resort; that includes works by Matisse, Rembrandt and Renoir, and most significantly Pablo Picasso's *Le Rêve*, purchased by Wynn in 1997 for £48.4 million.

Sensational performance For a memorable experience, try not to miss the *Le Rêve* spectacular—an aquatic show that dazzles with its extraordinary acrobatic feats, amazing sound and light effects and superb choreography.

THE BASICS

www.wynnlasvegas.com

➕ E7

✉ 3131 Las Vegas Boulevard South

☎ 702/770-7000

◷ Waterfall spectacular at regular intervals throughout the day and evening; *Le Rêve* Thu–Mon shows at 7 and 9.30

🍴 Several restaurants and cafés

🚍 Las Vegas Convention

🚍 Deuce

♿ Waterfall show free; *Le Rêve* very expensive

HIGHLIGHTS

● Waterfall and lagoon
● Lake of Dreams
● Art collection
● Ferrari-Maserati showroom
● *Le Rêve* show

More to See

THE ARTS FACTORY

www.theartsfactory.com

A complex at the heart of the 18b Las Vegas Arts District. Talented local artists are showcased across some 25 galleries and studios. This is the main venue for First Friday, held on the first Friday of each month. Galleries stay open late, artists display their work and street bands perform.

F4 ✉ 107 East Charleston Boulevard ☎ 702/676-1111 🕐 Times vary; some areas are closed to the public 🚌 Deuce; free bus service between First Friday stops 👆 Free

AN EVENING AT THE CAGE

www.rivierahotel.com

A cast of male impersonators transform into unbelievably accurate representations of female superstars such as Madonna or Cher.

E7 ✉ Riviera, 2901 Las Vegas Boulevard South ☎ 702/794-9433 🕐 Nightly 7.30pm 🚌 Deuce 👆 Very expensive

FASHION SHOW MALL

www.thefashionshow.com

Following a $362 million expansion, this mall is one of the country's largest and the city's premier retail destination. It is anchored by popular department stores Macy's (▷ 80) and Neiman Marcus and the structure enclosing the mall is known as the Cloud, acting as shade during the day and a movie screen at night.

D7 ✉ 3200 Las Vegas Boulevard South ☎ 702/784-7000 🕐 Mon–Sat 10–9, Sun 11–7 🍴 Numerous restaurants and cafés 🚌 Deuce

TRUMP HOTEL LAS VEGAS

www.trumplasvegashotel.com

At 64-stories high this is the city's tallest residential building and it has exterior windows gilded in 24-carat gold. Opened 2008, it is the creation of business magnate and international celebrity Donald Trump, housing a mix of hotel suites and residential condominiums. There's no casino here but the restaurant and cocktail bar, DJT (▷ 82), has a good reputation.

D7 ✉ 2000 Fashion Show Drive ☎ 702/982-0000 🍴 Restaurant 🚌 Deuce

Indulge yourself at Fashion Show Mall with its vast array of stores

Shopping

ABERCROMBIE & FITCH

www.abercrombie.com
A range for young aspiring men and women that features the company's preppy-style look in hoodies, sweats, shirts and jeans.
➕ D7 ✉ Fashion Show Mall, 3200 Las Vegas Boulevard South ☎ 702/650-6509 🚌 Deuce

BEBE

Sassy boutique selling sleek designs and curve-hugging wear inspired by the latest trends.
➕ D7 ✉ Fashion Show Mall, 3200 Las Vegas Boulevard South ☎ 702/892-8083 🚌 Deuce

BETSEY JOHNSON

Flowing fabrics with beaded and embroidered detail are the style at this wacky shop for a wacky clientele.
➕ D7 ✉ Fashion Show Mall, 3200 Las Vegas Boulevard South ☎ 702/735-3338 🚌 Deuce

BONANZA GIFTS

www.worldslargestgiftshop.com
The self-styled "largest souvenir store in the world" has a mind-boggling array of tacky mementos. It's worth a visit, just to see how tasteless it can all get.
➕ E6 ✉ 2440 Las Vegas Boulevard South ☎ 702/385-7359 🚌 Deuce

MACY'S

www.macys.com
The choice is extensive; all your fashion needs, for men, women and children, are here as well as accessories, shoes and home ware.
➕ D7 ✉ Fashion Show Mall, 3200 Las Vegas Boulevard South ☎ 702/731-5111 🚌 Deuce

MANOLO BLAHNIK

Timeless and beautifully made, Manolo's sexy shoes are as famous as the women who wear them.
➕ E7 ✉ Wynn Las Vegas, 3131 Las Vegas Boulevard South ☎ 702/770-7000 🚌 Deuce

OSCAR DE LA RENTA

This renowned designer, famous for his delicate and opulent collections of women's clothes and accessories, has chosen the Wynn Esplanade to display his finery.
➕ E7 ✉ Wynn Las Vegas, 3131 Las Vegas Boulevard South ☎ 702/770-7000 🚌 Deuce

JUST FOR FUN

There's no doubt about it, Las Vegas is chock-full of enough tacky souvenirs to be able to supply the rest of the world's major tourist spots. But this is Vegas after all, and kitsch is just another facet of its fun character. You can bet that not many people will leave without at least one item packed in their suitcase that announces to the world they have visited Sin City.

SAM ASH

www.samashmusic.com
A musicians' playground, stacked high with guitars, amps, drums and brass and wind instruments of every conceivable brand.
➕ H6 ✉ 2747 Maryland Parkway ☎ 702/734-0007 🚌 109

SERGE'S SHOWGIRL WIGS

www.showgirlwigs.com
Offering around 10,000 wigs, in all shapes and shades. Top one with a showgirl headdress.
➕ G6 ✉ Commercial Center Plaza, 953 East Sahara Avenue ☎ 702/732-1015 🚌 204

TEAVANA

www.teavana.com
Tea heaven and a must for all aficionados of the brew. There are white, black and green varieties, plus organic, herbal and many more. The teapots, mugs and storage tins make ideal gifts.
➕ D7 ✉ Fashion Show Mall, 3200 Las Vegas Boulevard South ☎ 702/369-9732 🚌 Deuce

WYNN ESPLANADE

An endless list of exclusive names at this luxury hotel mall. Take your pick from the likes of Manolo Blahnik and Louis Vuiton or the Ferrai-Maserati dealership.
➕ E7 ✉ Wynn Las Vegas, 3131 Las Vegas Boulevard South ☎ 702/770-7000 🚇 Las Vegas Convention Center 🚌 Deuce

Entertainment and Nightlife

B BAR
www.wynnlasvegas.com
The B Bar offers the perfect escape to indulge in nouvelle cocktails, fine wines and spirits before heading off to the casino for a flutter.
➕ E7 ✉ Wynn Las Vegas, 3131 Las Vegas Boulevard South ☎ 702/770-7000 🚌 Deuce

CASBAR THEATER LOUNGE
www.saharavegas.com
This is a real throwback to the Las Vegas of the 1970s, before any of today's sophistication set in. There's live entertainment nightly.
➕ F6 ✉ Sahara, 2535 Las Vegas Boulevard South ☎ 702/737-2111 🚋 Sahara 🚌 Deuce

COMEDY CLUB
www.rivierahotel.com
Four acts a night do stand-up at this comedy spot on the second floor of the Mardi Gras Plaza at the Riviera. Once a month the venue holds a late-night show for X-rated comedians.
➕ E6 ✉ Riviera, 2901 Las Vegas Boulevard South ☎ 702/794-9433 🚌 Deuce

CONGO SHOWROOM
www.saharavegas.com
A lively schedule of musicians and comedians is on the bill here.
➕ F6 ✉ Sahara, 2535 Las Vegas Boulevard South ☎ 702/737-2111 🚋 Sahara 🚌 Deuce

LAS VEGAS HILTON
www.lvhilton.com
A variety of musicians, comedians and magicians perform here and tickets are reasonably priced.
➕ F7 ✉ Las Vegas Hilton, 3000 Paradise Road ☎ 702/732-5755 🚋 Las Vegas Hilton 🚌 108

PEPPERMILL'S FIRE SIDE LOUNGE
www.peppermilllasvegas.com
Shag carpeting, fire pits, enormous white silk flowers and indoor fountains are still the rage at this tribute to old-world Vegas.
➕ E7 ✉ 2985 Las Vegas Boulevard South ☎ 702/735-4177 🚌 Deuce

ROMANCE AT THE TOP OF THE WORLD
www.stratospherehotel.com
Visit this sophisticated lounge bar before or after a meal at the Top of the World Restaurant (▷ 82). High up on the 107th floor, it has great city views. You can sip a cocktail in the inimate surroundings while listening to live music and relaxing in the snazzy leopard and leather chairs.
➕ F5 ✉ Stratosphere, 2000 Las Vegas Boulevard South ☎ 702/380-7705 🚌 Deuce

TRYST
www.wynnlasvegas.com
Rapidly becoming one of the most enticing nightclubs in the city, tantalizing Tryst sets a new trend for nightlife in Las Vegas. Sophisticated deep-red and black combinations enhance intimate booth-style seating and the open-air, sizable dance floor extends into a 90-ft (27m) waterfall that cascades into a lagoon.
➕ E7 ✉ Wynn Las Vegas, 3131 Las Vegas Boulevard South ☎ 702/770-3375 🚌 Deuce

VEGAS INDOOR SKYDIVING
www.vegasindoorskydiving.com
Test your skills at this exciting new sporting challenge. A vertical wind tunnel simulates the freefall experience of skydiving in a column of air with vertical air-speeds up to 120mph (193kph). No experience is needed; you can book a single flight session or a personalized coaching program.
➕ F7 ✉ 200 Convention Center Drive ☎ 702/731-4768 🚋 Las Vegas Hilton 🚌 108, Deuce

---

HEADLINERS

Headliners come and go in the city, some staying longer than others. But Las Vegas likes to keep its future big names under wraps, so you never know what's lined up. Recent superstars who have performed here include U2, Paul McCartney and Barry Manilow. As shows can close just like that, it is always best to check before turning up.

NORTH STRIP

ENTERTAINMENT AND NIGHTLIFE

Restaurants

DANIEL BOULUD BRASSERIE ($$$)

www.wynnlasvegas.com
Chef Daniel Boulud
brings his mastery of
French cuisine to this
bustling brasserie over-
looking the lagoon. Be
sure to reserve for a seat
on the coveted patio.
➕ E7 ✉ Wynn Las Vegas,
3131 Las Vegas Boulevard
South ☎ 702/248-DINE
🕐 Daily 5.30–10.30
🚌 Deuce

DJT ($$$)

www.trumplasvegashotel.com
Named after the initials
of the Trump Hotel's
illustrious owner, Donald
Trump, this restaurant
offers fine dishes crafted
by chef John Jay Watson,
inspired by his class
French training and
Southern heritage.
➕ D7 ✉ 2000 Fashion
Show Drive ☎ 702/476-7358
🕐 Breakfast daily 6.30–11,
lunch daily 11.30–2, dinner
Tue–Sun 5–10 🚌 Deuce

ENVY ($$$)

www.envysteakhouse.com
Richard Chamberlain, one
of America's leading
chefs, uses top-quality
fresh ingredients in his
innovative dishes, which
redefine the traditional
steak-house offerings.
Soothing red shades give
a sophisticated feel.
➕ F7 ✉ Renaissance, 3400
Paradise Road ☎ 702/784-
5716 🕐 Daily 6.30–3, 5–10
(Fri, Sat until 10.30) 🚌 Las
Vegas Hilton 🚌 108

KRISTOFER'S ($$)

www.rivierahotel.com
The great steaks, tender
ribs and broiled chicken
in butter served here are
matched by great prices;
the barbecue sauce is
wonderful, too.
➕ E6 ✉ Riviera, 2901 Las
Vegas Boulevard South
☎ 702/794-9233 🕐 Daily
5–10 🚌 Deuce

LOTUS OF SIAM ($)

www.saipinchutima.com
One of only a few Thai
restaurants in Las Vegas,
with a huge menu of
dishes. Let them know
how hot you like your
food and they'll prepare it
accordingly. If you overdo
it, have the coconut ice
cream for dessert.

DINING WITH A VIEW

There are some wonderful
spots in Vegas where you can
savor great views while you
eat, but one of the best is the
Top of the World restaurant
(▷ this page). Located on
the 106th floor of the
Stratosphere Tower, it makes
one revolution in 60 minutes,
during which you can see the
Strip, the mountains, the
valleys and beyond.

➕ G6 ✉ 953 East Sahara
Avenue ☎ 702/735-3033
🕐 Mon–Fri 11.30–2.30, 5.30–
9.30, Sat, Sun 5.30–10 🚌 204

RA ($$)

www.rasushi.com
An upbeat, casual mood
creates the perfect setting
to enjoy fresh sushi,
Japanese-fusion cuisine
and signature dishes so
good that you can't wait
to return. Bright wall
hangings and globe light-
ing accent the interior.
➕ D7 ✉ Fashion Show Mall,
3200 Las Vegas Boulevard
South ☎ 702/696-0008
🕐 Daily 11–midnight
🚌 Deuce

THE STEAK HOUSE ($$)

www.circuscircus.com
This old-timer is popular
for its succulent prime
ribs and tasty grilled
steaks, all at low prices.
There's seafood, lobster,
chicken and lamb as well.
➕ E6 ✉ Circus Circus, 2880
Las Vegas Boulevard South
☎ 702/794-3767 🕐 Sun–Fri
5–10, Sat 5–11 🚌 Deuce

TOP OF THE WORLD ($$$)

www.topoftheworldlv.com
Enjoy high end, delicious
culinary creations in
this revolving restaurant
833ft (254m) above
the Strip.
➕ F5 ✉ Stratosphere Tower,
2000 Las Vegas Boulevard
South ☎ 702/380-7711
🕐 Sun–Thu 11–3, 5.30–10.30,
Fri, Sat 11–3, 5.30–11
🚌 Deuce

Evolving from the early saloons, the first casino-hotels were built downtown in the 1930s. Now, in the shade of the booming Strip, projects such as the Fremont Street Experience have helped it keep pace.

Downtown

HIGHLIGHTS

- Fremont Street Experience (▷ 88)
- Main Street Station
- Golden Nugget Casino (▷ 90)
- The Arts Factory

TIP

- Some of the carts around Fremont have unusual gift items for sale.

With its old-world appeal, Downtown is where the spirit of Las Vegas's humble beginnings still lives on through original casino hotels like the Plaza, Golden Nugget and Golden Gate.

Origins Centered on Fremont Street between Main and 9th, the streets of Downtown are narrower, more low-key and less glamorous than the Strip. In the 1920s, Fremont Street was the first street in Las Vegas to be paved and have traffic lights, and by the 1930s it had the first licensed gaming hall. Downtown already had 36 years of history as the commercial heart of Vegas by the time the first casino resort, El Rancho, was built on the Strip in 1941.

Revitalization Downtown had lost much of its business to the Strip by the 1990s, when Vegas

Mermaids Casino (top left); historic Downtown hotels such as the Golden Gate (top right, below right) and the Plaza (below middle left) are an interesting reminder of the city's frontier history; antique slot machine (below middle right) and detail of a glass window (below left), both displayed at the Golden Gate

entrepreneur Steve Wynn and fellow hoteliers set about reinventing the area. They came up with the $70 million Fremont Street Experience (▷ 88), which succeeded in bringing in the punters once again and putting Glitter Gulch—as it is known— firmly back on the map.

More attractions With its striking Victorian decor and genuine antiques, Main Street Station (▷ 109) has one of the city's best casinos in terms of comfort and atmosphere, and it's smoke-free. Just outside Main Street Station two old rail cars are displayed. One is the Blackhawk used by Buffalo Bill Cody to travel with his Wild West Show between 1906 and 1917 and still in its original state. The other, the Cascade, is a wonderfully preserved Pullman car built in 1897, complete with original lamps, wood paneling and ornate mirrors.

THE BASICS

🏠 G2
✉ Centered around Fremont and Main streets
🍴 Numerous
🚌 108, Deuce

Fremont Street Experience

Fremont Street ablaze after dark (left); Fremont hotel, a Downtown institution (right)

THE BASICS

www.vegasexperience.com

✚ G3

✉ Fremont Street

☎ 702/678-5600

🕐 Shows at 8.30, 9, 10, 11 and midnight

🚌 108, Deuce

✋ Free

DID YOU KNOW?

● Fremont Street was the hub of Las Vegas for nearly four decades.
● Each column supporting the overhead structure carries 400,000lb (181,440kg) of weight.
● The components for the light show produce 65,536 color combinations.
● The show's sound system generates 540,000 watts.

Head north to the Downtown area after dark to see the only show of its kind in the world—a fantastic light-and-sound show on a massive frame that overarches a five-block area.

High-tech marvel The specifications for the initial display comprised 2 million light bulbs, with strobe lighting added to enhance the disco nights. In 2004, a $17 million upgrade provided a 12.5 million LED light display and a better quality sound system (to 550,000 watts) for state-of-the-art sound. The Experience is a high-tech phenomenon with the latest computers intertwining the light, visual and audio systems.

Under cover of lightness This glittering spectacular is based on a huge, solid frame that curves 90ft (27m) above traffic-free Fremont Street, between Main and 4th streets, covering an area of more than 4 acres (1.5ha). A number of the Downtown casinos are within this area, adding to the overall effect with their illuminated facades. There are 16 massive columns and 43,000 struts supporting the frame, but once the show starts you are totally focused on this breathtaking experience that has been wowing the crowds—some 19 million in 2006—here since 1995.

By day You might suppose that, by comparison, it's rather dull here during the day. But the display frame shelters a lively shopping mall, the sound system continues to pipe in music to shop by, and there are often free concerts and street performers.

Las Vegas Natural History Museum

This terrific museum provides a welcome contrast to the high life and glitz of the shows and casinos. There are lots of interactive displays, live animals to pet, animatronic dinosaurs and much more.

Unique items When you consider all the museums in the United States, you might not expect a Las Vegas institution to have something the others don't. However, among the displays here are two particularly rare species—the African water chevrotain (a cross between a pig and a deer) and the Liberian zebra duiker. In addition, there are more than 26 species of stuffed animals mounted in cases, including the largest jaguar ever displayed.

Marine world Opened in 2004, the whales exhibit is part of the Marine Life Gallery and complements the shark displays featuring live leopard sharks and a shark egg hatchery. There is a scale model of an orca, also known as the killer whale, a melonhead whale and a beluga whale, complete with baby. You can learn about the behavior and conservation of these creatures. Don't miss the re-creation of the jaws of a 50ft-long (15m) prehistoric shark.

Fun with the animals Many of the displays are animated, including five robotic dinosaurs—the 35ft (10.5m) T-rex is very popular. There are also live animals that visitors are occasionally allowed to pet. The concept is to combine education with fun, and the interactive area is a great place for children to try out their skills as amateur archeologists and paleontologists.

THE BASICS

www.lvnhm.org
 H2
✉ 900 North Las Vegas Boulevard
☎ 702/384-3466
🕐 Daily 9–4
🚌 113
✋ Moderate

HIGHLIGHTS

● Hands-on activity room
● Whales exhibition
● Marine Life Gallery
● Robotic T-rex and Dinosaur Gallery
● African Galleries

DOWNTOWN

TOP 25

More to See

GOLDEN NUGGET
www.goldennugget.com
One of Las Vegas's original casinos, built in 1946, the Golden Nugget was given a $170 million refurbishment between 2006 and 2008. The star attraction is The Tank—a central water feature complete with a shark tank. Slide down a transparent tube through the middle of the tank to get a closer view of its residents.
➕ G3 ✉ 129 East Fremont Street
☎ 702/ 385-7111 🕐 Daily 24 hours
🚌 108, Deuce

LIED DISCOVERY CHILDREN'S MUSEUM
www.ldcm.org
Constantly changing exhibits introduce children to the wonders of science, technology and the environment.
➕ H2 ✉ 833 Las Vegas Boulevard North
☎ 702/382-3445 🕐 Tue–Fri 9–4, Sat 10–5, Sun 12–5 🚌 113 ❗ Inexpensive

NEON MUSEUM
www.neonmuseum.org
This is, in fact, an outdoor self-guided walking tour on and around Fremont Street. Some of the city's famed neon signs dating back to 1940 are displayed as installation artworks on, or just off, Fremont Street. Call for details.
➕ G3 ✉ Fremont Street ☎ 702/387-6366 🚌 108, Deuce ❗ Free

OLD MORMON FORT
www.parks.nv.gov/olvmf.htm
The first people to settle the area were Mormons, who built a fort here in the mid-19th century. They turned to farming, but were driven out in 1858 by frequent Native American raids. The Vistor Center tells their story with displays and historic artifacts.
➕ H2 ✉ 500 East Washington Avenue
☎ 702/486-3511 🕐 Daily 8–4.30 (closed Sun and Mon in winter) 🚌 113 ❗ Inexpensive

VEGAS VIC AND VEGAS VICKI
These nostalgic neon signs are part of Downtown's history; Vic is perched on top of the Pioneer Club and Vicki on the Girls of Glitter Gulch.
➕ G3 ✉ Fremont Street 🚌 108, Deuce

The elegant Golden Nugget hotel casino

Begin just as dusk falls, walking through a historic part of the city past some of the early buildings, and finishing in a blaze of neons.

DISTANCE: 1 mile (1.5km) **ALLOW:** 2 hours

START ....

EL CORTEZ HOTEL
✚ G3 🚌 108, Deuce

.... **END**

EAST FREEMONT
✚ G3 🚌 108, Deuce

1 Start at El Cortez, the only Downtown property whose exterior has remained mostly unaltered. Turn right onto Las Vegas Boulevard. Take the 2nd left onto Stewart Avenue.

2 About halfway up on the right is the Post Office/Federal Building–a neoclassical structure built in 1933. Continue to the top and at T-junction with Main Street you will see Main Street Station hotel (▷ 109).

3 Pick up a map at the front desk and take a self-guided tour of the antiques collection. Continue along Main Street. On the right is an antique rail car that served as a personal car for Buffalo Bill Cody and Annie Oakley (▷ 87).

4 Next on the right you come to the Union Plaza hotel, where the Union Pacific Railroad Depot stood, once the focal point of Downtown.

8 Cross over Las Vegas Boulevard to Fremont East; a developing entertainment district where you can view more antique neon signs.

7 Stay for the light-and-sound show before proceeding to the end. At the intersection with Las Vegas Boulevard are refurbished signs, such as Aladdin's Lamp and the Hacienda Horse and Rider, from the Neon Museum collections (▷ 90).

6 Turn down Fremont Street (▷ 88) under the huge canopy. Look out for the neon signs Vegas Vic and Vegas Vicki (▷ 90). Farther down is the Golden Nugget (▷ 90), Binion's and the Fremont, three of Downtown's most nostalgic hotel casinos.

5 Cross the road to the Golden Gate, one of the oldest remaining hotels in the area.

Shopping

99 CENT ONLY STORE
www.99only.com
Las Vegas isn't all designer shops and expensive boutiques. Take a look at this huge store where literally everything is just 99 cents. With a boom in sales at branches across the country, the store stocks groceries, beauty products, household supplies and gifts.
✚ H4 ✉ 1155 East Charleston Boulevard ☎ 702/382-1882 🚌 206

THE ATTIC
www.atticvintage.com
There is a hidden treasure in every corner in this fascinating place, including a good range of retro and vintage clothing, interesting collectibles, furniture, jewelry, old radios, TVs, cameras and electrical appliances.
✚ F3 ✉ 1018 South Main Street ☎ 702/388-4088 🚌 108

THE FUNK HOUSE
www.thefunkhouselasvegas.com
One of the best antiques stores in the city is the creation of Cindy Funkhouser. Her growing collection includes some interesting items from the late-1950s and early-1960s including furniture, glass, jewelry, rugs, paintings and toys. Enjoy browsing.
✚ F4 ✉ 1228 South Casino Center Boulevard ☎ 702/678-6278 🚌 105, 108, 116

GAMBLER'S GENERAL STORE
www.gamblersgeneralstore.com
What better souvenir of a trip to Las Vegas than something with a gambling theme? Take home a roulette wheel, blackjack table or slot machine. The used-card decks and gambling chips from major casinos are good, inexpensive buys.
✚ F3 ✉ 800 South Main Street ☎ 702/382-9903 🚌 108

LAS VEGAS PREMIUM OUTLETS
www.premiumoutlets.com
Save 25 to 65 percent at this 120 designer and name-brand outlet, names include: Ann Taylor, Dolce and Gabbana, Guess, Adidas and Elie Tahari.

CULTURAL CORRIDOR
On Las Vegas Boulevard between Bonanza Road and Washington Avenue is a hub of seven institutions that promote art and history in the city. The Cashman Center, an arts and sporting center; Las Vegas Library; Natural History Museum (▷ 89); Lied Discovery Children's Museum (▷ 90); Neon Museum (▷ 90); Old Mormon Fort (▷ 90); and the Reed Whipple Cultural Center, which encourages local, regional and national artists. For more information visit www.culturalcorridorvegas.org

✚ F3 ✉ 875 South Grand Central Parkway ☎ 702/474-7500 🚌 108, 109 from DTC

MAIN STREET ANTIQUES
www.mainstreetantiqueslv.com
This large store on two floors, offers treasures from some 40 dealers. Lots of Vegas collectibles can be found, plus items from around the world. Check out the rare items from the 1950s and 1960s.
✚ F3 ✉ 500 South Main Street ☎ 702/382-1882 🚌 108

RAINBOW FEATHER DYEING COMPANY
www.rainbowfeatherco.com
A shrine to the feather. Feathers of every hue and shade are made into boas, ornaments and jewellery, as well as flights for archery. Master feather-crafter Bill Girard creates wonderful accessories, which are worn by Las Vegas showgirls and Cirque du Soleil acrobats.
✚ F3 ✉ 1036 South Main Street ☎ 702/598-0988 🚌 108

SILVER HORSE ANTIQUES
Take a look at this fascinating store, with lamps, furniture, glass collectibles and other items hidden in a real treasure house.
✚ H4 ✉ 1651 East Charleston Boulevard ☎ 702/385-2700 🚌 206

Restaurants

BINION'S COFFEE SHOP ($)

www.binions.com
A great place for a light snack or something more substantial at a low price. The generous breakfasts are particularly good.
✚ G3 ⊠ Binion's, 128 Fremont Street ☎ 702/382-1600 🕐 Daily 24 hours 🚌 108, Deuce

BINION'S RANCH STEAKHOUSE ($$$)

www.binions.com
Settle down to the delicious succulent steaks and chops that are served amid the attractive Victorian decor, while taking in the spectacular views of Las Vegas.
✚ G3 ⊠ Binion's, 128 East Fremont Street ☎ 702/382-1600 🕐 Daily 5–11 🚌 108, Deuce

DONA MARIA TAMALES ($)

www.donamariatamales.com
Certainly best here are the great *tamales*—shredded chicken, beef and pork wrapped in cornmeal.
✚ G4 ⊠ 910 Las Vegas Boulevard South ☎ 702/382-6538 🕐 Mon–Fri 8–10, Sat, Sun 8–11 🚌 Deuce

GARDEN COURT ($)

www.mainstreetcasino.com
Watch your food being prepared at what is said to be Downtown's best buffet. Choices include Mexican, Asian and American plus specialty nights such as T-bone Tuesday.
✚ G2 ⊠ Main Street Station, 200 North Main Street ☎ 702/387-1896 🕐 Mon–Fri 7–10.30, 11–3, 4–10, Sat, Sun 4–10 🚌 108, Deuce

HUGO'S CELLAR ($$$)

www.hugoscellar.com
Below street level, this romantic restaurant has a touch of class. Each woman receives a red rose as she enters the low lit, dark-wood space. Excellent Continental cuisine; some dishes are prepared at the table. Expect lots of pampering.
✚ G3 ⊠ Four Queens Hotel, 202 Fremont Street ☎ 702/385-4011 🕐 Daily 5–11 🚌 108, Deuce

LILLIE'S NOODLE HOUSE ($$)

www.goldennugget.com
There's an odd mix of cultures at work here, but the cuisine is most definitely Chinese, and the Sichuan and Cantonese dishes are of exceptional quality.
✚ G3 ⊠ Golden Nugget, 129 East Fremont Street ☎ 702/385-7111 🕐 Sun–Thu 5–midnight, Fri–Sat 5–1am 🚌 108, Deuce

SECOND STREET GRILL ($$)

www.fremontcasino.com
Step back in time at this hidden gem and sample good Pacific rim and contemporary cuisine at affordable prices. Soft lighting and rich woods encourage you to relax in the oversized chairs.
✚ G3 ⊠ 200 Fremont Street ☎ 702/385-3232 🕐 Sun, Mon, Thu 6–10, Fri, Sat 6–11.30 🚌 108, Deuce

TRIPLE GEORGE GRILL ($$–$$$)

www.triplegeorgegrill.com
A popular joint, this sophisticated grill offers reliable quality steaks, fine seafood dishes, yummy desserts and a remarkable service. Portions are big so you may want to share a dish.
✚ G3 ⊠ 201 North Third Street ☎ 702/384-2761 🕐 Mon 11–4, Tue–Fri 11–10, Sat 4–10 🚌 108, Deuce

Farther Afield

Just a short distance from Vegas there is a different world of great natural beauty. Its geological formations, spectacular scenery and varied wildlife are light years away from the razzmatazz.

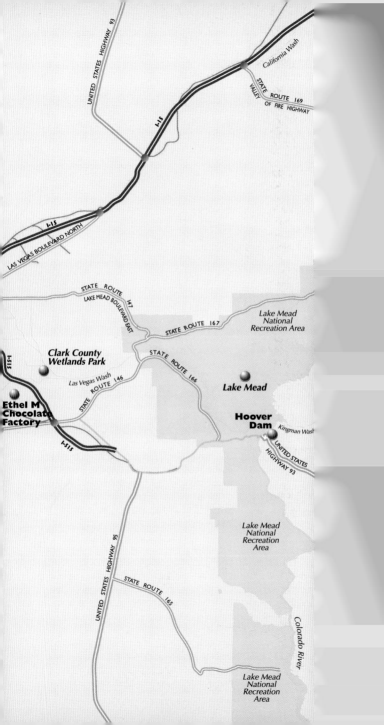

Hoover Dam and Lake Mead

HIGHLIGHTS

● Guided tour into the Hoover Dam
● Cruising Lake Mead on an organized sightseeing tour

TIPS

● There is a large choice of tours available from Las Vegas (▷ 119).
● The best sightseeing cruise on Lake Mead is the one aboard the *Desert Princess*.
● Tours of the dam leave from the exhibit center at the top of the dam.

It's hard to visit Vegas without feeling some wonderment about the power it must take to light up the town. You'll find some answers at Hoover Dam, and while you're out of the city, enjoy a cruise on the lovely lake it created.

A marvel of engineering Without the Hoover Dam, Las Vegas, as we know it, would not exist. Constructed in the mid-1930s to control flooding on the Colorado River, it also provides drinking water for 25 million people and electricity for half a million homes. It was a massive undertaking that was, amazingly, completed two years ahead of schedule. At the peak of construction, over 5,000 people were employed and 96 workers died on the project. Fascinating tours take visitors deep inside the structure to learn about its inner workings.

Hoover Dam's structural volume surpasses that of the largest pyramid in Egypt (left); Lake Mohave, encompassed in the Lake Mead National Recreation Area (below middle); men at work—the dam is considered one of the seven engineering wonders of the world (top middle); fireworks over Lake Mead (right)

Lovely Lake Mead The damming of the Colorado River between 1935 and 1938 created the second-largest artificial lake in the United States, with a vast 550-mile (885km) shoreline. There's a scenic drive along the western side, and the Alan Bible Visitor Center, just west of the dam, has lots of useful information about waterborne activities. There are five marinas, and you can rent a boat or jet ski, do some fishing, go water-skiing or swimming. On dry land there are lakeshore walks and facilities for camping and picnicking. A great way to see the lake is from one of the many available boat trips, which include breakfast, lunch, dinner and dinner-dance cruises. Boulder City, on the lake shore, is an interesting place that was built to house dam construction workers and was "dry" (no alcohol or gambling). It is the only community in Nevada that still restricts gambling.

THE BASICS

www.usbr.gov/lc/hoover dam; www.nps.gov/lame
➕ Off map at J1
✉ 30 miles (48km) southeast of Las Vegas
☎ Hoover Dam tours: 702/494-2517; Alan Bible Visitor Center: 702/293-8990; Lake Mead Cruises: 702/294-6180
🕐 Hoover Dam Visitor Center: daily 9–4; Alan Bible Visitor Center: daily 9–4.15
♿ Hoover Dam Visitor Center Tours: moderate–expensive. Lake Mead Recreation Area: inexpensive; Lake Mead cruise: expensive

Red Rock Canyon

HIGHLIGHTS

● Scenic Drive
● Hiking trails
● Children's Discovery Trail
● Wildlife—burros (wild donkeys) and mountain lions (hard to spot)

TIPS

● Don't feed the wildlife; the burros may bite or kick.
● Take plenty of water if hiking—the heat can be fierce—and wear extra layers in winter.

This canyon was created 65 million years ago when the Keystone Thrust Fault pushed one rock plate up over another. The resulting spectacular formations, in contrasting gray limestone and red sandstone, are awesome.

Focal point It's incredible to think that this striking canyon, set in the 197,000-acre (79,725ha) Red Rock Canyon National Conservation Area, is a mere 20-minute drive from the razzmatazz of Vegas. The focal point is the steep red rock escarpment more than 13 miles (21km) long and almost 3,000ft (915m) high. More canyons have been gouged out within the formation by constant snowmelt and rains, creating the present dramatic landscape. In contrast to the dry desert, springs and streams encourage lush vegetation.

Whatever way you choose to travel through Red Rock Canyon, on foot, by car or bicycle, there are breathtaking vistas all around

Planning ahead The best place to start is at the Red Rock Visitor Center, which offers information and interpretation about all the recreational opportunities available, including hiking and climbing. It also has a recorded self-guide tour giving you a description of the geology and wildlife (all protected) in the area, and provides maps of hiking and bicycle trails and details of picnic sites. Park rangers are also on hand to give advice. Climbing should be undertaken only by experts with the correct equipment. Stick to the trails and be aware of weather conditions—flash floods do occur.

Loop the loop For those staying in their cars, the 13-mile (21km) one-way Scenic Drive, leaving from the Visitor Center, gives the chance to see some of the best rock formations and to pause for photos at the Calico Vista viewpoints.

THE BASICS

www.nv.blm.gov/
redrockcanyon
➕ Off map at A4
✉ South Nevada,
20 miles (32km) west of
Las Vegas
☎ Red Rock Visitor
Center: 702/515-5350
🕐 Red Rock Visitor
Center: daily 8–4.30
🅿 Parking: inexpensive;
free for hikers

More to See

CLARK COUNTY WETLANDS PARK

www.accessclarkcounty.com/parks
Just 8 miles (13km) east of the strip, this environmentally concious park has a visitor center where you can pick up trail maps. Bird-watching is popular here, with species that include great blue herons, snowy egrets and black bellied whistling ducks.
🞣 Off map at J10 ✉ 7050 Wetlands Park Lane ☎ 702/ 455-7522 ⏰ Visitor Center: daily 9–3; Nature Center: daily dawn–dusk 🚍 202, then walk 1 mile (1.5km) ✋ Free

ETHEL M. CHOCOLATE FACTORY

www.ethelschocolate.com
Take a self-guiding audio tour to discover how Ethel Mars's chocolate enterprise began and get an insight into the production processes. At the end sample your favorite candy.
🞣 Off map at J11 ✉ 2 Cactus Garden Drive, Henderson (8 miles/5km southeast of Las Vegas) ☎ 702/435-2655 ⏰ Daily 8.30–6 (factory not operational on Sun) 🚍 217 ✋ Free

NEVADA STATE MUSEUM

Learn about life before Vegas, and view exhibits of dinosaurs and early man right through to the controversial nuclear testing program. Photographic displays of Las Vegas in the early years are on show. Due to move to the Springs Preserve (see below) in 2010.
🞣 B2 ✉ 700 Twin Lakes Drive ☎ 702/ 486-5205 ⏰ Daily 9–5 🚍 106, 208 ✋ Inexpensive

SPRINGS PRESERVE

www.springspreserve.org
Springs Preserve is set in 180 acres (73ha) on the site of the original water source for Las Vegas, which dried up in 1962. Learn more about desert living through interactive displays and exhibits. There are 8-acres (3ha) of botanical gardens and walking trails
🞣 B3 ✉ 333 South Valley View Boulevard ☎ 702/822-7700 ⏰ Daily 10–6 🍴 Springs Café 🚍 201, 202, 204 from Strip, disembark at Valley View Boulevard stop and take bus 104 north to Meadows Mall ✋ Moderate; gardens and trails free

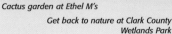

Cactus garden at Ethel M's
Get back to nature at Clark County Wetlands Park

Excursions

THE BASICS

www.nps.gov/grca
Distance: South Rim 260 miles (418km) from Las Vegas; North Rim 275 miles (443km)
✉ South Rim Visitor Center: opposite Mather Point (about 4 miles/6.5km north of the south entrance station). North Rim Visitor Center: opposite parking lot on Bright Angel Peninsula
🕐 South Rim Visitor Center: daily 8–5 (longer during peak times). North Rim Visitor Center: mid-May to mid-Oct daily 8–6
❓ It is best to take an organized tour. Many companies offer bus, helicopter and light aircraft trips from Las Vegas

GRAND CANYON

To stand on the rim of the Grand Canyon and look down to its floor a mile below is to be confronted with raw nature at its most awe-inspiring. It's a sight from which any number of neck-craning fellow tourists can never detract.

The Grand Canyon stretches some 277 miles (446km) along the course of the Colorado River, and it is this mighty river that created it, eroding the landscape over a period of 5 million years. This erosion has revealed layer upon twisted layer of limestone, sandstone and shale, a fascinating geological cross-section of the earth's crust. At its widest point it is 17 miles (27km) from one side to the other and its deepest point is 1 mile (1.6km) beneath the rim.

The South Rim, 260 miles (418km) from Las Vegas, is the more touristy side of the canyon, because it's more accessible, with an airport and rail depot. Grand Canyon Village here also has lots of visitor facilities, including hotels, restaurants, shops and museums. In addition, this is the start point for treks down into the canyon; if you have the energy this is a wonderful way to appreciate the topography to the full.

If you really want to get away from the crowds and experience the vast emptiness of the canyon, head for the incredibly spectacular North Rim, about 275 miles (443km) from Las Vegas in the dense forest of the Kaibab Plateau. If you want to visit both the North Rim and South Rim, you will need to figure into your travel plans the additional 200 miles (320km) it takes to get from one side to the other.

VALLEY OF FIRE STATE PARK

Nevada's first state park takes its name from its red sandstone rock formations, formed millions of years ago by a shift in the earth's crust and eroded by water and wind.

The resulting weird and wonderful shapes resemble everything from elephants to pianos. Note the ancient rock art (*petroglyphs*) by the prehistoric Basketmaker people and Anasazi Pueblo farmers, who are thought to be North America's earliest inhabitants living along the Muddy River between 300BC and AD1150. The park also offers an opportunity to enjoy activities such as hiking, rock hunting, camping and picnicking. The visitor center provides trail maps and information.

THE BASICS

www.parks.nv.gov/vf.htm
Distance: 55 miles (88km) northeast of Las Vegas
Journey Time: 1 hour
✉ Visitor Center: SR169 in Overton
☎ 702/397-2088
🕐 Daily 8.30–4.30
🅿 Parking inexpensive
❓ Take an organized tour or go by car via I-15 from Las Vegas

MOUNT CHARLESTON

Only a short drive away and always cooler than Las Vegas—by as much as 40°F (22°C)—this lovely alpine wilderness is an absolute joy to visit.

Located in the Spring Mountains, Charleston's peak reaches 11,900ft (3,628m). Together with the surrounding Toiyabe Forest, it is popular for hiking (52 miles/84km of trails), picnicking and camping. Nearby Lee Canyon is a great spot for skiing. Thick bristlecone pines cling to the limestone cliffs forming an awesome backdrop. The US Forest Service maintains the marked trails, which are suitable for all abilities. At the top of Kyle Canyon is the Mount Charleston Lodge, where you can enjoy good food and live entertainment in front of an open fire, with breathtaking views. When there is enough snow, horse-drawn sleighs leave from here.

THE BASICS

Distance: 35 miles (56km) northwest of Las Vegas
Journey Time: 30 mins
❓ Take an organized tour or go by car (check road conditions in winter). From Las Vegas, take I-15 west and continue to US95 north. Stay on 95 until Kyle Canyon Road, then follow signs to Mount Charleston

FARTHER AFIELD

EXCURSIONS

Valley of Fire State Park

Shopping

BOULEVARD MALL
www.boulevardmall.com
The oldest mall in Las Vegas, popular with customers in the southeast of the city for its moderate price tags. It has some 140 shops including department stores JC Penney, Macy's and Sears.
✚ H8 ✉ 3528 Maryland Parkway ☎ 702/732-8949
🚌 109

CHINATOWN PLAZA
www.lvchinatown.com
More than 25 vendors can be found in this red-roof Asian shopping mall, selling ceramics, clothing and handmade furniture.
✚ Off map ✉ 4255 Spring Mountain Road ☎ 702/221-8448 🚌 203

HARLEY-DAVIDSON
www.lvhd.com
The world's largest Harley store with a vast array of merchandise and bikes on display. Rent a bike here if you can't afford to buy.
✚ J6 ✉ 2605 South Eastern Avenue ☎ 702/431-8500
🚌 110

JANA'S JADE GALLERY
This gallery sells an unusual and fascinating selection of hand-crafted jade jewelry.
✚ Off map ✉ Chinatown Plaza, 4255 Spring Mountain Road ☎ 702/227-9198
🚌 203

MEADOWS MALL
www.meadowsmall.com
Yet another huge mall made up of more than 140 main-street names and department stores.
✚ B2 ✉ 4300 Meadows Lane (at intersection of Valley View and US95) ☎ 702/878-3331 🚌 103, 104, 402

TOWN SQUARE
Colonial and Spanish-style facades, enhanced by antique streetlights, conceal an eclectic mix of stores, restaurants and bars. A small central park houses a children's playground and picnic area. There is a cinema on site.
✚ D12 ✉ 6605 Las Vegas Boulevard South ☎ 702/269-5000 🕐 Mon–Thu 10–9.30, Fri–Sat 10–10, Sun 11–8
🍴 Numerous restaurants and cafés 🚌 104, Deuce

Entertainment and Nightlife

ANGEL PARK GOLF CLUB
www.angelpark.com
Experience both mountains and palms at this 36-hole course designed by legendary golfer Arnold Palmer. There are views over Red Rock Canyon.
✚ Off map ✉ 100 South Rampart Boulevard, west of US95 at Summerlin Parkway
☎ 702/254-4653

LAS VEGAS NATIONAL
www.lasvegasnational.com
Opened in 1961, this classic 18-hole golf course has glistening lakes. In 1996, champion golfer Tiger Woods won his first PGA victory here.
✚ J7 ✉ 1911 Desert Inn Road ☎ 702/734-1796
🚌 213

ORLEANS ARENA
www.orleansarena.com
Since opening in 2004, this huge arena has hosted Disney on Ice, top concerts and a variety of sporting events.
✚ A10 ✉ Orleans, 4500 West Tropicana ☎ 702/365-SHOW; tickets 702/284-7777 🚌 201

ROYAL LINKS GOLF CLUB
www.royallinksgolfclub.com
This course has holes based on holes from famous British Open courses. In keeping with the British theme, the 18th hole looks like a medieval castle.
✚ Off map ✉ 5995 East Vegas Valley Road, 6 miles (10km) east ☎ 702/450-8123

A big part of the Las Vegas experience is to stay in one of the resort hotels. There is an endless supply of hotel rooms in the city and most of the biggest hotels in the world are here.

Introduction

Las Vegas is one of the few cities in the world where you can eat, drink, shop and be entertained without even needing to leave your hotel.

Hotels

For a truly unique experience, stay in one of the theme casino hotels on and around the Strip. These are like no others in the world and give you the added benefit of being right in the heart of the action. An increasing number of smaller, more exclusive hotels are popping up that offer an alternative for those who want time out away from the neon jungle. The north end of the Strip has seen better days in places. Some bastions of the "Golden Era" remain and have undergone extensive renovations, while others are gradually being torn down to make way for dazzling new resorts. If you want a taste of nostalgia, choose a hotel in historic Downtown, which still remains a favorite with millions of visitors.

Motels

Las Vegas boasts dozens of motels near the Strip and downtown. Rates can be rock-bottom and their rooms are normally the last to get booked up, making them a good bet for finding a last-minute room. Motels don't have casinos, which also means they don't have large crowds. Don't expect much more than standard motel lodgings, but if you are on a tight budget and only require a clean, comfortable place to sleep, a motel is ideal.

GETTING THE BEST DEAL

For the best deal start looking well in advance: In Las Vegas it really does pay to shop around. Set a budget, know where you would like to stay and in what type of accommodations. Generally, prices are lower during the week but room rates fluctuate according to demand—they can change from day to day. Check to see if the city is staging a major convention before deciding when to go, as accommodations will be in demand, making prices higher. If you do your homework first, it's possible to get a luxury hotel room at a budget price.

Las Vegas tempts you to live in the lap of luxury with prices you can't refuse

Budget Hotels

BALLY'S LAS VEGAS

www.ballyslasvegas.com
More sedate than many Vegas hotels, Bally's is less oriented toward a lively young crowd or families. The 2,814 rooms and 265 suites are sumptuous, with grand sitting rooms and opulent bathrooms. Floodlit tennis courts.
➕ D9 ✉ 3645 Las Vegas Boulevard South ☎ 702/739-4111; fax 702/967-4405
🚃 Bally's/Paris 🚌 Deuce

CIRCUS CIRCUS (▷ 72)

www.circuscircus.com
Although it is one of the oldest hotels on the Strip, after recent refurbishments Circus Circus still provides one of the best value-for-money options if you have kids with you. It has 3,770 rooms and 130 suites.
➕ E6 ✉ 2880 Las Vegas Boulevard South ☎ 702/734-0410; fax 702/794-3816
🚌 Deuce

FAIRFIELD INN LAS VEGAS AIRPORT

www.fairfieldinn.com
Only two blocks east of the Strip, this pristine, small—in Vegas terms—hotel has a contemporary design. The 129 family rooms have a living area and are decorated in cheerful hues. Start your day with the "Early Eats" complimentary breakfast. Outdoor swimming pool and fitness center.
➕ F8 ✉ 3850 Paradise Road ☎ 702/791-0899; fax 702/791-2705 🚌 108

FLAMINGO LAS VEGAS

www.flamingolasvegas.com
Bugsy Siegel's original 1946 Flamingo was rebuilt by the Hilton group in 1993. The modern hotel has 3,565 units in all; the deluxe king rooms are spacious. The Flamingo also has one of the best pool areas on the Strip.
➕ D9 ✉ 3555 Las Vegas Boulevard South ☎ 702/733-3111; fax 702/733-3528
🚃 Flamingo/Caesars
🚌 Deuce

HAWTHORN SUITES

www.hawthorn.com
An appealing alternative if you prefer some distance

between you and the Strip, but not too far off the beaten track. A good choice for families; the suites are plain but have kitchens and a balcony, and lots of extras. There are 71 rooms.
➕ Off map ✉ 910 Boulder Highway, Henderson ☎ 702/568-7800; fax 702/568-8430 🚌 217

MAIN STREET STATION

www.mainstreetcasino.com
This characterful hotel has a Victorian theme, with genuine antiques, flickering gas lamps, iron railings and stained-glass windows. It has 406 bright rooms.
➕ G2 ✉ 200 North Main Street ☎ 702/387-1896
🚌 108

SOMERSET HOUSE

Handy for the Convention Center, and one block off the Strip, this good-value motel has 104 rooms and minisuites.
➕ E5 ✉ 294 Convention Center Drive ☎ 702/735-4411; fax 702/369-2388
🚃 Las Vegas Convention Center 🚌 108, Deuce

TERRIBLE'S

www.herbstgaming.com
Don't be fooled by the name, as this small hotel near the Strip is anything but terrible. The 374 pleasant rooms are basic but clean, at very agreeable rates.
➕ F9 ✉ 4100 Paradise Road ☎ 702/733-7000; fax 702/691-2415 🚌 108

Mid-Range Hotels

PRICES

Expect to pay between $120 and $200 per night for a double room in a mid-range hotel.

ALEXIS PARK

www.alexispark.com
If you prefer to stay off the Strip, this small hotel, with 495 rooms, has some great two-level suites for a really good price. It's also fairly quiet here. Facilities include a spa.

➕ E9 ✉ 375 East Harmon Avenue ☎ 702/796-3300; fax 702/796-0766 🚌 108

COURTYARD BY MARRIOT

www.courtyard.com/LASCH
Part of the well-known chain, this hotel provides 149 nicer-than-the-average motel rooms (including 12 suites).

➕ F7 ✉ 3275 Paradise Road ☎ 702/791-3600; fax 702/796-7981 🚌 108

EMERALD SUITES – LAS VEGAS BLVD

www.emeraldsuites.com
On the Strip south of the Mandalay Bay, this non-gaming establishment features 396 suites, both one and two bedrooms, each tastefully decorated and equipped with a fully fitted kitchen. Guests have use of a lagoon-style pool nestled in pleasant landscaping.

➕ Off map ✉ 9145 Las Vegas Boulevard South ☎ 702/948-9999; fax 702/948-9998 🚌 117

EXCALIBUR (▷ 24)

www.excalibur.com
Kids love this medieval castle, with its moat and drawbridge. Parents might find it all just a little tacky, but it's probably the best deal on the Strip, and has 3,991 comfortable, peaceful rooms.

➕ D10 ✉ 3850 Las Vegas Boulevard South ☎ 702/597-7777; fax 702/597-7009 🚌 Deuce

HOOTERS

www.hooterscasinohotel.com
It's all surfboards and palm trees at this recently remodeled casino-hotel.

THE HOTEL EXPERIENCE

The fanciful hotel architecture of Las Vegas means that many people come here for the hotel experience alone. Some rarely leave the premises—quite understandable when there's an on-site casino, a choice of superb restaurants, world-class shows and shopping, luxury spas and plenty of other leisure amenities. On the downside, the large hotels can suffer from slow service and long lines for checking in and out, though express check-out boxes are available in many cases. You simply drop off your keys and leave, and your credit card is charged about a week later. If you are going to stay in a very large hotel, try to get a room near the elevator.

Floridian-style bedrooms, some in a bungalow building separate from the main towers, are bright and sunny. Hooters is more intimate than some of the Vegas giants and has a fun atmosphere and friendly staff. Over 650 rooms.

➕ D10 ✉ 115 East Tropicana ☎ 702/739-9000; fax 702/736-1120 🚌 201

HOWARD JOHNSON –LAS VEGAS STRIP

www.howardjohnson
lasvegasstrip.com
This low-rise motel is in a good location at the north end of the Strip. Some of the 100 rooms have a whirlpool bath.

➕ F5 ✉ 1401 Las Vegas Boulevard South ☎ 702/388-0301; fax 702/388-2506 🚌 Deuce

LAS VEGAS HILTON

www.lvhilton.com
This old-timer still offers fine accommodations in its 3,000 guest rooms, with individual opulent style. Elvis staged his comeback here in 1969 to 1977 (note the statue at the entrance), and the hotel was used in the Bond film *Diamonds are Forever*.

➕ F7 ✉ 3000 Paradise Road ☎ 702/732-5111; fax 702/732-5948 🚌 Las Vegas Hilton 🚌 108

LUXOR (▷ 28)

www.luxor.com
This 4,400-room hotel may have moved away from its Egyptian theme

but you still enter beneath a huge sphinx and are taken to your room via an elevator that travels up the slope of the pyramid.

🔲 D11 ✉ 3900 Las Vegas Boulevard South ☎ 702/262-4444; fax 702/262-4452 🚌 Deuce

MGM GRAND
www.mgmgrand.com
This is pure Hollywood, with figures of stars dotted around the lobby and huge stills from movies on the walls. The 5,000-plus rooms offer a range of options, from the small Emerald Tower rooms to large spacious suites.

🔲 D10 ✉ 3799 Las Vegas Boulevard South ☎ 702/891-1111; fax 702/891-3036 🚇 MGM Grand 🚌 Deuce

MONTE CARLO (▷ 36)
www.montecarlo.com
A popular choice with golfers (it has a full-time golf concierge), the Monte Carlo has 3,000-or-so attractive rooms and suites.

🔲 D10 ✉ 3770 Las Vegas Boulevard South ☎ 702/730-7777; fax 702/730-7250 🚌 Deuce

NEW YORK-NEW YORK (▷ 31)
www.nynyhotelcasino.com
Love it or hate it, this huge mock-up of the New York skyline is an experience to stay at. The 2,023 rooms are in a sophisticated '40s-style decorated in earth tones and pastels. Light sleepers should request a room away from the roller-coaster that trundles around the outside.

🔲 D10 ✉ 3790 Las Vegas Boulevard South ☎ 702/740-6969; fax 702/740-6920 🚌 Deuce

PALMS RESORT
www.palms.com
As the name suggests, expect plenty of tropical foliage at this towering hotel. The Palms' hot-spot reputation is due mainly to the clientele attracted to its nighttime haunts, such as the Ghostbar (▷ 64), attract. The 700 bedrooms are luxurious, with huge bathrooms.

🔲 B9 ✉ 4321 West Flamingo Road

HOTEL TIPPING
As in any US city, it is customary to offer a gratuity to hotel employees for prompt and courteous service. Las Vegas has a huge amount of different staff who provide such services, and who gets what can be confusing. The amount is at the customer's discretion but here are some general guidelines: bell captains and bellhops $1–$2 per bag; hotel maids $2 per day upon departure; valets $2; use of concierge or VIP services $5; waiters and waitresses 15 to 20 percent of the bill.

☎ 702/942-7777; fax 702/942-7001 🚌 202

RIO ALL-SUITE HOTEL
www.riolasvegas.com
This is a lively hotel in an off-Strip location, with great nightlife and two excellent buffets among its dining options. It has 2,548 huge suites.

🔲 B8 ✉ 3700 Flamingo Road ☎ 702/777-7777; fax 702/777-7611 🚌 202

TREASURE ISLAND (TI)
www.treasureisland.com
This hotel has left behind its Pirates of the Caribbean swashbuckling image for a more sophisticated adult take on the highseas. The 3,000 rooms and suites, decorated in French Regency style, have floor-to-ceiling windows—Strip side, there's no better view of the Sirens of TI pirate battle (▷ 61).

🔲 D8 ✉ 3300 Las Vegas Boulevard South ☎ 702/894-7111; fax 702/894-7446 🚌 Deuce

THE VENETIAN (▷ 56)
www.venetian.com
Famous for its canals and replica of St. Mark's Square, the Venetian has 4,027 rooms (actually they are all suites). The decor varies, although all have marble bathrooms and fine furnishings.

🔲 D8 ✉ 3355 Las Vegas Boulevard South ☎ 702/414-1000; fax 702/414-1100 🚌 Deuce

Luxury Hotels

BELLAGIO (▷ 46)

www.bellagio.com
Set behind an enormous lake, this is one of the most beautiful hotels in Vegas, built in the style of a huge Mediterranean villa with lovely gardens. The 3,933-plus rooms and suites are large and classy, decorated in natural hues.
➕ D9 ✉ 3600 Las Vegas Boulevard South ☎ 702/693-7111; fax 702/693-8559
🚌 Deuce

CAESARS PALACE (▷ 47)

www.caesarspalace.com
Ancient Rome prevails through classical temples, marble columns and every possible excess you can imagine. All 3,300 rooms and suites are luxurious, but even more so in the tower, with huge whirlpool tubs in the bathroom.
➕ D8 ✉ 3570 Las Vegas Boulevard South ☎ 702/731-7110; fax 702/697-5706
🚌 Deuce

FOUR SEASONS LAS VEGAS

www.fourseasons.com
This hotel takes up the top five levels of the Mandalay Bay, but retains its own tranquil identity. The 424 rooms and suites are elegantly decorated in peach, aqua and gold, and all the

Mandalay Bay facilities are available to guests.
➕ D11 ✉ 3960 Las Vegas Boulevard South ☎ 702/632-5000; fax 702/632-5195
🚌 Deuce

MANDALAY BAY

www.mandalaybay.com
There is masses of big-city style at the Mandalay Bay. It's the only hotel in Las Vegas with a beach and a gigantic wave pool. There are 3,200-plus rooms and suites; even the standard rooms are huge, and all are light and airy.
➕ D11 ✉ 3950 Las Vegas Boulevard South ☎ 702/632-7777; fax 702/632-9215
🚌 Deuce

PLATINUM HOTEL AND SPA

www.theplatinumhotel.com
Opened July 2006, this non-gaming retreat is in lavish contemporary style. The spacious 255 one-

and two-bedroom suites have a kitchen, whirlpool tubs and a balcony overlooking the Strip or mountains. Make use of the soothing spa or indoor and outdoor pools.
➕ D9 ✉ 211 East Flamingo Road ☎ 702/365-5000; fax 702/365-5001 🚌 202

RENAISSANCE LAS VEGAS

www.renaissancelasvegas.com
For a retreat from the Vegas clamor and commotion, the Renaissance has cool and confident style without a slot machine in sight. The 578 rooms and suites are richly decorated and have a calming feel. Swimming pool, whirlpool and fitness center.
➕ F8 ✉ 3400 Paradise Road ☎ 702/784-5700; fax 702/735-3130 🚌 Las Vegas Convention Center 🚌 108

WYNN LAS VEGAS (▷ 77)

www.wynnlasvegas.com
Steve Wynn's latest incredible hotel-casino is one of the world's most expensive hotels, and occupies 60 floors. The 2,716-plus rooms are huge, very stylish, and are equipped with every conceivable luxury. There is a private lake, man-made mountain and an 18-hole golf course.
➕ E7 ✉ 3131 Las Vegas Boulevard South ☎ 702/770-7000; fax 702/770-1571 🚌 Las Vegas Convention Center
🚌 Deuce

A trip to Las Vegas can be hectic so it is best to organize as much as you can before you leave. The following information will help in planning transportation, reserving tours and making the best use of time in the city.

Planning Ahead

When to Go

With so many of its attractions under cover and not dependent on weather conditions, there's no off-season to speak of in Las Vegas. Avoid high summer if you don't like excessively hot weather, unless you plan to stay indoors.

TIME

Vegas is on Pacific Standard Time (GMT −8), advanced one hour between early April and early October.

AVERAGE DAILY MAXIMUM TEMPERATURES

JAN	FEB	MAR	APR	MAY	JUN	JUL	AUG	SEP	OCT	NOV	DEC
56°F	62°F	68°F	78°F	88°F	98°F	104°F	102°F	94°F	81°F	66°F	57°F
13°C	17°C	20°C	25°C	31°C	36°C	40°C	39°C	34°C	27°C	19°C	14°C

Summer (June to September) can be incredibly hot and oppressive, with daytime temperatures sometimes soaring as high as 120°F (49°C).

Spring and autumn are much more comfortable, with average temperatures usually reaching 70°F (21°C).

Winter (December to February) sees average temperatures above 50°F (10°C). There can be the odd chillier day when you will need a jacket, and sometimes it can drop below freezing at night.

WHAT'S ON

January *Laughlin Desert Challenge*: Top drivers compete in an off-road motor race over rough terrain.

March *NASCAR Nextel Cup Race* (early Mar): A major event on the racing calendar, held at the Las Vegas Motor Speedway.

St. Patrick's Day Parade (Mar 17): A parade of floats downtown kicks off other entertainment; Celtic bands, storytellers and dancers.

June *CineVegas International Film Festival* (early Jun): Film debuts from studios, with celebrities attending the huge parties.

Jul/Aug *World Series of Poker*: The world's best poker players compete for supremacy at Harrah's Rio.

September *International Mariachi Festival*: A popular Mexican festival that takes place at the Paris Theatre, Paris Las Vegas hotel.

October *Frys.com Open*: A major week-long golf tournament played on two of the city's best courses.

November *Comedy Festival*: A festival in multiple venues throughout Caesars Palace, with dozens of performers and special events.

December *National Finals*

Rodeo (early Dec): During the 10-day finals, cowboys compete and Vegas goes country-mad, dressing up, line-dancing and barbecuing.

New Year's Eve Celebrations: A party held at Fremont Street.

Billboard Music Awards: Music celebrities gather at the MGM Grand Garden Arena to honor the world's best music.

First Friday A huge arts and entertainment party takes place on the first Friday of each month in the Arts District downtown (✉ 702/384-0092; www.firstfriday-lasvegas.org ⏰ 6–10pm).

Las Vegas Online

www.visitlasvegas.com
The official website of the Las Vegas Convention and Visitors Authority offers well-presented information on everything you need to know when planning your trip to Las Vegas.

www.lasvegas.com
For articles on local news, listings, events and other sources of information, try this useful site run by the respected *Review Journal*, Nevada's largest newspaper.

www.vegas.com
This informative site geared to visitors has honest reviews of restaurants, bars, shows and nightlife, and gives access to hotel booking.

www.lasvegasgolf.com
To help you plan a golfing holiday in Las Vegas, this site has detailed reviews on all the courses open in Vegas and other US cities.

www.vegasexperience.com
This lively site is dedicated to the Fremont Street Experience. See what's going on at any time of the year and look for places to stay and eat.

www.gayvegas.com
The most complete site for gay locals and visitors to Las Vegas. It keeps up with the latest information on clubs, bars, restaurants and organizations, plus lots more.

www.nightonthetown.com
For one of the most comprehensive and easy-to-use guides to eating out in Las Vegas, check out this site. The restaurants are listed under cuisine type and location.

www.cheapovegas.com
Geared to the visitor who wants to do Vegas on a budget, this fun guide provides comprehensive reviews and unbiased opinions with a humorous slant.

PRIME TRAVEL SITES

www.rtcsnv.com/transit/
Official site for theRegional Transportation Commission of Southern Nevada (RTC)), the company responsible for the Las Vegas bus system. Use the transit system map, routes and schedule pages to discover exactly how to get from A to B.

www.fodors.com
A complete travel-planning site where you can research prices and weather; book air tickets, cars and rooms; pose questions (and get answers) to fellow visitors; and find links to other sites.

INTERNET ACCESS

Most hotels in Las Vegas have business centers and offer internet access to their guests but you have to be aware that most hotels charge very high prices for internet access, and for WiFi connection when using your own laptop. It is possible to find free access in some hotels but you will need to enquire on arrival or look online. Try:
http://.govegas.about.com
For cafés try:
www.cybercafes.com up-to-date search engine enabling you to locate internet cafés all over the world.

Getting There

ENTRY REQUIREMENTS

Visitors to the US must show a full passport, valid for at least six months. You will need to complete an Electronic System of Travel Authorization (ESTA™) before traveling to the USA. ESTA™ is a web-based system and can only be accessed online. For more information, and to complete the ESTA™ form visit https://esta.cbp.dhs.gov. Most UK citizens and visitors from other countries belonging to the Visa Waiver Program can enter without a visa, but you must have a return or onward ticket. Regulations can change, so always check before you travel with the US Embassy (☎ 020 7499 9000; www.usembassy.org.uk)

AIRPORT FACTS

● McCarran airport has two well-organized terminals with around 55 retail shops and nearly 50 restaurants and snack bars.
● It has recently undergone a $500 million expansion.
● 47 million passengers per year pass through the airport.
● It is among the 15 busiest airports in the world.
● This is one of only a few airports where you can play the slot machines while waiting for your luggage, or visit the 24-hour fitness center.

AIRPORT

McCarran International Airport (LAS) is served by direct flights from cities right across North America, and there are intercontinental flights from London, Frankfurt and Tokyo. It is worth checking for special deals from airline and flight brokers, in newspapers and on the internet.

FROM MCCARRAN INTERNATIONAL AIRPORT

The McCarran airport terminal (☎ 702/261-5211; www.mccarran.com) is 4 miles (6km) southeast of the Strip, at 5757 Wayne Newton Boulevard. There is a ground Transportation Center near baggage claim for shuttles and for renting cars and limousines and information desks can be found throughout the airport.

Several companies run airport shuttle buses every 10 or 15 minutes from just outside the baggage claim area—leave through door exits 7–13. They all cost roughly the same (about $6.50 to the Strip and $8 to Downtown) and normally operate 24 hours. Most stop at all the major hotels and motels. Advance reservations for shuttles ☎ 702/558-9155. Check first, as your resort hotel might offer an airport shuttle. Less expensive are the CAT buses (about $1.25 one way) that operate from outside the airport terminal: No. 108 will take you to the Las Vegas Hilton, from where you can transfer to the Deuce (▷ 118), which stops close to most hotels along the Strip; and No. 109 goes to the Downtown Transportation Center.

Taxis are easily available outside baggage claim, and cost $8.20 to the Strip, or $20 to Downtown hotels (depends on traffic and destination). Stretch limos line up outside the airport waiting to take you to your destination; if you are tempted, try to share as they can be costly ($55 up to $125 per hour, depending on the size). Try Ambassador Limousines (☎ 702/362-6200) or Las Vegas Limousines (☎ 702/948-7714). For car rentals, all major car rental companies are represented inside the airport's arrival hall (▷ panel). There are buses and shuttles available to take you to the rental company you are using. It is better to reserve a car in advance.

ARRIVING BY BUS
Greyhound/Trailways (www.greyhound.com) operates services to Las Vegas from most cities and towns in California and Nevada. Tickets can be purchased just prior to departure. This is a convenient and inexpensive way to travel, although not the most comfortable. All Greyhound buses arrive at Downtown's bus terminal at 200 South Main Street (☎ 702/384-9561).

ARRIVING BY CAR
Interstate 15 from Los Angeles to Vegas takes you through some of the most breathtaking scenery of the Mojave Desert. The journey takes 4–5 hours depending on road, weather and traffic conditions (delays often caused by construction work). Carry plenty of water and a spare tire, and keep an eye on your fuel level.

ARRIVING BY RAIL
Amtrak, the national train company, does not offer a direct service to Las Vegas. You can connect to the city by bus from other rail destinations in California and Arizona. Amtrak has talked of restoring the line from Los Angeles to Las Vegas, but at the time of writing nothing had materialized. Contact Amtrak (☎ 800/872-7245; www.amtrak.com) for the latest details.

CAR RENTAL

Hotel information desks can advise about renting a car. Rental companies will deliver to hotels and pick up at the end of the rental period.

Avis	702/531-1500
Budget	702/736-1212
Enterprise	702/795-8842
Hertz	702/262-7700
National	702/263-8411
Thrifty	702/896-7600

There is a centralized rent-a-car center at McCarran Airport serviced by all the major rental companies. All customers will be transported to their vehicles by dedicated shuttles. For information, call 702/261-6001.

CUSTOMS

● Visitors from outside the US, 21 or over, may import duty-free: 200 cigarettes, or 50 non-Cuban cigars, or 2kg of tobacco; 1 liter of alcohol; and gifts up to $100 in value.
● Imports of wildlife souvenirs sourced from rare or endangered species may be illegal or require a special permit. Check your home country's customs rules.
● Restricted import items include meat, seeds, plants and fruit.
● Some medication bought over the counter abroad may be prescription-only in the US and could be confiscated. Bring a doctor's certificate for essential medication.

Getting Around

VISITORS WITH DISABILITIES

If you are a wheelchair-user, on arrival at the airport you will find shuttle buses with wheelchair lifts to get you into the city. You will also find easy access to most restaurants, showrooms and lounges. All the hotel casinos have accessible slot machines, and many provide access to table games. Assisted listening devices are also widely available. If you plan to rent a car, you can request a free 90-day disabled parking permit, which can be used throughout Vegas; contact the City of Las Vegas Parking Permit Office (☎ 702/229-4700).
Las Vegas Convention and Visitors Authority ADA coordinator
☎ 702/892-0711

WALKING

The Strip is 3.5 miles (5.5km) long, and it's a taxing walk in the heat. Wear comfortable shoes and sunglasses. Even if you use the Strip's transportation, you will still have to walk considerable distances to and from the hotels and attractions. Overhead walkways connect several places along the Strip. Make a note of the cross streets that punctuate the Strip to help get your bearings; some are named after the hotels along them.

Most of what you will want to see and do in Las Vegas is found along Las Vegas Boulevard, which is well served by buses. The boulevard is divided into two parts: Downtown, between Charleston Boulevard and Washington Avenue; and the Strip, comprising several long blocks—Sahara, Spring Mountain, Flamingo, Tropicana and Russell. Hotels on the Strip (between Hacienda Avenue and the Sahara Hotel) are also served by red and green Las Vegas Strip Trolleys, and in 2004 the first leg of a new multimillion dollar monorail was launched, providing a welcome addition to the options for getting up and down the Strip.

BUSES

CAT, Citizens Area Transit, run by the RTC (Regional Transportation Commission (▷ 115) of Southern Nevada) ☎ 702/228-7433 runs 51 bus routes throughout the entire system, of which 24 operate 24 hours a day. The Downtown Transportation Center (DTC) at Casino Center Boulevard and South Strip Transfer Terminal (SSTT) at Gillespie Street are major transfer points. The Deuce provides transportation along the Strip from the DTC to the SSTT, with many stops along the way, and runs about every 10 minutes (during peak times) 24 hours a day. The double-decker bus, launched in 2005, accommodates 97 people. The fare is $2 one-way or $5 for a day pass, which you can purchase on the bus or from vending machines (you need to have the exact fare because drivers can't give change). You can get a transfer from the driver for off-Strip destinations, so you don't have to pay again. Off-strip buses otherwise cost $1.25 one-way. Hotels should have timetables for the citywide system; if not, call the number above.

DRIVING

Almost every hotel on Las Vegas Boulevard South has its own self-parking garage. The best way into these garages, avoiding the gridlock on the Strip, is via the back entrances. Valet

parking is also available at the front (and sometimes other) entrances. The standard tip for valets is $2 if they are particularly speedy. The best advice about driving in Las Vegas is don't do it unless you really have to. The speed limit on the Strip is 35mph (56kph). The wearing of seat belts is compulsory.

MONORAILS
The eagerly awaited state-of-the-art monorail (www.lvmonorail.com) opened in 2004. Running from MGM Grand to the Sahara, it operates every day from 7am to 2am (Fri, Sat until 3am). There are seven stations: MGM Grand, Bally's/Paris, Flamingo/Caesars, Harrah's/Imperial Palace, Las Vegas Convention Center, Las Vegas Hilton and Sahara. A single fare costs $5, an unlimited one-day pass is $12 and an unlimited three-day pass costs $28. There are also a number of smaller free monorail services courtesy of the hotels, including one between the Mandalay Bay, the Excalibur and the Luxor (every 3–7 minutes, 24 hours), and one between the Mirage and Treasure Island every 5–15 minutes (9am–midnight).

TAXIS AND LIMOUSINES
Taxis line up outside every hotel and can be called from your room. When out, you need to call or go to a cab stand; taxis can't be hailed in the street. Taxi drivers have first-hand experience of all the shows and attractions, and can offer a review and make recommendations. For this service you should give more of a tip than the standard $1 or $2 for a straightforward journey. Also give a bigger tip if they help with the door and your luggage. There are plenty of limousine services, which start at $38 ($55 for a stretch limo) per hour. Your hotel concierge can make the necessary arrangements.
Suggested taxi companies:
ACE Cab Co. 702/736-8383; Checker Cab 702/873-2000; Western Cab Co. 702/736-8000 Limousine Company: Ambassador Limousine 702/362-6200 (toll free 1-888 519-5466).

ORGANIZED SIGHTSEEING
There is no shortage of Vegas-based tour companies offering trips from Vegas to wherever you want to go, but there are also plenty showing the best of the city sights. These tours can give you an insider's view on city attractions, along with a good overview and orientation, before you start exploring independently. Nearly every hotel in Las Vegas has a sightseeing desk from where you can book tours. If the tour bus approach doesn't appeal to you, there are all kinds of other options, including small-scale specialized tours with your own group of family or friends, or using a limousine to whisk you from place to place. Perhaps best of all, you can take to the skies in a helicopter for a bird's-eye view of the fantastic architecture and, on after-dark flights, the glittering lights. Also after dark, nightclub tours the Nitelife Tour Company's (www.nite-tourslasvegas.com) will transport you to the current most popular dance and Latin clubs. The company also offers personalized tours to suit all tastes. Other reputable tour companies include Scenic Airlines (www.scenic.com) and Look Tours (www.looktours.com).

Essential Facts

In medical emergencies call ☎ 911 or go to the casualty department of the nearest hospital. Emergency-room services are available 24 hours at University Medical Center (✉ 1800 West Charleston Boulevard ☎ 702/383-2000), or Sunrise Hospital and Medical Center (✉ 3186 Maryland Parkway ☎ 702/731-8000). Pharmacies are indicated by a large green or red cross. Pharmacy telephone numbers are listed under "Pharmacies" or "Drugstores" in the Yellow Pages. Many will deliver medication to your hotel. 24-hour and night pharmacies are available at Walgreens (✉ 1111 Las Vegas Boulevard ☎ 702/471-6840), and at Sav-On (✉ 2300 East Tropicana Avenue ☎ 702/736-4174).

ELECTRICITY

● Voltage is 110/120 volts AC (60 cycles) and sockets take two-prong, flat-pin plugs. European appliances also need a voltage transformer.

EMERGENCIES

Police ☎ 911
Fire ☎ 911
Ambulance ☎ 911
American Automobile Association (AAA) breakdown service ☎ 800/222-4357.

ETIQUETTE

● Tip staff at least 15–20 percent in a restaurant, taxi drivers $1–$2 for a direct route, porters $1–$2 per bag, depending on the distance carried, and valet parking attendants $2.
● Las Vegas is one of the few pro-smoking places left in the US. Most restaurants have designated smoking areas.
● Dress is very informal during the day, and shorts and T-shirts are generally accepted anywhere. In the evening, smart-casual is more the norm, and some lounges, nightclubs and restaurants may have a dress code.

GAMING

Nevada law permits a wide variety of gaming, but the most popular flutters are roulette, blackjack, craps and slot machines. If you are new to the game, spend some time watching before actually taking the plunge; you could pick up a few tips from the hard-and-fast gamblers. Punters have to be 21 to play. Most casinos do not have windows or clocks, so you are unaware of time passing, and they will often keep you refueled with free drinks and snacks. One benefit of all this cash changing hands is that most of the gaming taxes collected by the state are funneled into public education.

Glossary of terms:
Action Gaming activity measured by the amount wagered.

Bank The person covering the bets in any game, usually the casino.
Buy in Purchasing of chips.
Cage The cashier's section of the casino.
Even money A bet that pays off at one to one.
House edge The mathematical advantage the casino enjoys on every game and wager.
House odds The ratio at which the casino pays off a winning bet.
Limit The minimum/maximum bet accepted at a gambling table.
Loose machine A slot machine set to return a high percentage on the money you put in.
Marker An IOU owed to the casino by someone playing on credit.
Toke A tip or gratuity.

LOST PROPERTY
● For property lost on public transportation: ✉ 6675 South Strip Transfer Terminal, South Gillespie Street ☎ 702/228-7433 ⏰ Mon–Fri 8–4.30.
● For property lost at McCarran International Airport: ☎ 702/261-5134 ⏰ Daily 6.30am–1am.
● Report losses of passports or credit cards to the police.

NATIONAL HOLIDAYS
Jan 1: New Year's Day
3rd Mon in Jan: Martin Luther King Jr. Day
3rd Mon in Feb: President's Day
Mar/Apr: Easter (half-day holiday on Good Friday)
Last Mon in May: Memorial Day
Jul 4: Independence Day
1st Mon in Sep: Labor Day
2nd Mon in Oct: Columbus Day
Nov 11: Veterans' Day
4th Thu in Nov: Thanksgiving
Dec 25: Christmas Day

OPENING HOURS
● Banks: generally Mon–Fri 9–3 or later, and some Sat mornings.

MONEY
● Credit cards are widely accepted.
● Most banks have ATMs.
● US-dollar traveler's checks are accepted as cash in most places, but ID may be requested.
● Most major hotels will exchange foreign currency, and there are several exchange bureaus on the Strip. You can also change money at major banks.

CURRENCY
The unit of currency is the dollar ($), divided into 100 cents. Bills (notes) are in denominations of $1, $5, $10, $20, $50 and $100. Coins are 1 cent (penny), 5 cents (nickel), 10 cents (dime), 25 cents (quarter) and 50 cents (half dollar).

5 dollars

10 dollars

50 dollars

100 dollars

NEWSPAPERS AND MAGAZINES

● Las Vegas has two daily newspapers: the *Las Vegas Review Journal* and the *Las Vegas Sun*.
● Weeklies with club listings and restaurant and bar reviews include *City Life* and *Las Vegas Weekly*.

TELEPHONE

There are public payphones in hotels, casinos, stores, restaurants, gas stations and on many street corners. You will need a good supply of quarters (overseas calls cost at least $5.50). Local calls from a phone booth cost around 50 cents. Some phones are equipped to take prepaid phone cards and/or charge cards and credit cards. Dial 1 plus the area code for numbers within the United States and Canada. Calls made from hotel rooms are very expensive. Las Vegas's area code is 702, which does not need to be dialed if you are calling within the city. To call Las Vegas from the UK, dial 00 followed by 1 (the code for the US and Canada), then the number. To call the UK from Las Vegas, dial 00 44, then drop the first zero from the area code.

● Post offices: normally Mon–Fri 8.30–6, with limited hours on Sat.
● Stores: usually open at 10am; closing times vary, and may be later on weekends.
● Museums: see individual entries for details.
● Las Vegas boasts that it never closes and never sleeps, but off-Strip stores and banks, and peripheral businesses, will be closed on certain holidays.

POST OFFICES

● Main post office: ✉ 1001 East Sunset Road, between Paradise Road and Maryland Parkway ☎ 702/361-9349 ⏲ Mon–Fri 8–9, Sat 8–4. There are many post offices in the city. You can also mail letters and parcels from your hotel.
● Buy stamps from shops and from machines.
● US mailboxes are red and white.

SENSIBLE PRECAUTIONS

Carry only as much money with you as you need; leave other cash and valuables in the hotel safe. At night, avoid hotel parking lots and always enter the hotel via the main entrance. If renting an apartment, use valet parking. Report theft or mugging on the street to the police department immediately. Make sure your room is locked when you leave. Locks can be changed regularly in hotels for security reasons.

STUDENT TRAVELERS

Discounts are sometimes available to students who have an International Student Identity Card (ISIC).

TOILETS

There is never a shortage of clean, free public restrooms to be found throughout the city in hotels, casinos, restaurants and bars.

TOURIST INFORMATION OFFICE

Las Vegas Visitor Information Center:
✉ 3150 Paradise Road, Las Vegas, NV 89109
☎ 702/892-7575 ⏲ Daily 8–5;
www.visitlasvegas.com

Language

The official language of the USA is English, and, given the large number of visitors from the UK, Las Vegas residents have few problems coping with British accents and dialects. Spanish is also widely spoken, as many workers in the hotel and catering industries are of Latin origin. Below is a selection of common UK English words with the US alternative on the right.

USEFUL WORDS	
shop	*store*
chemist (shop)	*drugstore*
cinema	*movie theater*
film	*movie*
pavement	*sidewalk*
subway	*underpass*
toilet	*restroom*
trousers	*pants*
nappy	*diaper*
glasses	*eyeglasses*
policeman	*cop*
post	*mail*
surname	*last name*
holiday	*vacation*
handbag	*purse*
cheque	*check*
banknote	*bill*
cashpoint	*automatic teller*
autumn	*fall*
ground floor	*first floor*
first floor	*second floor*
flat	*apartment*
lift	*elevator*
eiderdown	*comforter*
tap	*faucet*
luggage	*baggage*
suitcase	*trunk*
hotel porter	*bellhop*
chambermaid	*room maid*
cupboard	*closet*
car	*automobile*
bonnet	*hood*
boot	*trunk*
petrol	*gas*

FOOD	
grilled	*broiled*
prawns	*shrimp*
aubergine	*eggplant*
courgette	*zucchini*
chips	*fries*
crisps	*chips*
biscuit	*cookie*
scone	*biscuit*
jelly	*jello*
jam	*jelly*
sweets	*candy*
soft drink	*soda*

Timeline

EARLY BEGINNINGS

In prehistoric times the land on which the city stands was a marshy area that supported vigorous plant life, but the water eventually receded and the arid landscape we see today was created. However, underground water occasionally surfaced to nourish an oasis on the site where Vegas now stands, known at that time only to the area's Native Americans. Archaeological finds just 10 miles (16km) northwest of Vegas have identified one of the oldest sites of human habitation in the United States. Items found at Tule Springs date from around 11,000 to 14,000 years ago.

1829 The spring at Las Vegas is discovered by a Mexican scout, Rafael Rivera, riding with a 60-strong trading party that had strayed from the Spanish Trail en route to Los Angeles.

1855 Mormon settlers build a fort at Las Vegas. They stay for three years, until Native American raids drive them out.

1905 On May 15, the railroad arrives, and trackside lots in what is now the Fremont Street area sell like hot cakes.

1910 Gambling is made illegal in the state of Nevada, sending the games underground.

1931 The Nevada legislature passes a bill to allow gambling, and El Rancho becomes the first casino to open in Las Vegas. Nevada remains the only state to allow casino gambling until 1976, when casinos are introduced to Atlantic City.

1940s A building boom expands Las Vegas and more casinos come to town, along with organized crime. Vegas is ruled by the Mafia for decades.

1946 The Flamingo, one of the foremost early casinos, opens its doors. It is financed by Benjamin "Bugsy" Siegel of the Meyer Lansky gang.

1959 The Tropicana Hotel buys the American rights to the Parisian Folies

Bergere show—it runs until 2009 with some 40,000 spectators a month.

1960s The Rat Pack (Frank Sinatra, Dean Martin, Sammy Davis Jr. et al.) come to Las Vegas, setting the pattern for superstar entertainment.

1967 The Nevada legislature approves a bill that allows publicly traded corporations to obtain gambling licenses. Legitimate money begins to loosen the Mafia's hold.

1976 Casino gambling is legalized in Atlantic City; Las Vegas has competition.

1990s Las Vegas begins to promote family attractions. Ever bigger, more fantastic architecture starts to dominate the Strip.

2001 Wayne Newton, "Mr Las Vegas," signs a lucrative contract with the Stardust Hotel.

2004 A new state-of-the art monorail opens.

2005 On May 15, Las Vegas celebrates its 100th birthday.

2007 Opened 1958, the legendary Stardust Hotel is the latest hotel to be demolished.

2009 The world economic downturn bites in Las Vegas. Casino projects are frozen, tourist numbers are down and there is an unemployment crisis.

EVERYONE A WINNER

The fortunes of Las Vegas owe a lot to entrepreneur and property developer Steve Wynn (b1942). Raised in a Jewish family in New York, he took over the family bingo business in the 1960s and moved to Las Vegas in 1967. His first major venture here was the total revamp of the Golden Nugget. His next project was the casino resort the Mirage, which opened in 1989, followed by Treasure Island in 1993. Next came Bellagio, spawning a new breed of luxury resorts. When his company Mirage Resorts was sold to MGM in 2000 he turned his energies to his most expensive development the Wynn Las Vegas, followed by the Encore nextdoor. Wynn became a billionaire by 2004 and is an ardent art collector.

From left to right: The Folies Bergere at the Tropicana; The Rat Pack hit the scene in the 1960s; the Desert Inn, an old favorite no longer standing; the early days of gambling

Index

CITYPACK TOP 25
Las Vegas

WRITTEN AND UPDATED BY Jackie Staddon and Hilary Weston
COVER DESIGN AND DESIGN WORK Jacqueline Bailey
INDEXER Marie Lorimer
IMAGE RETOUCHING AND REPRO Sarah Montgomery and James Tims
PROJECT EDITOR Jennie Liscombe
SERIES EDITOR Marie-Claire Jefferies

© **AA MEDIA LIMITED 2010**

First published 2006
New edition 2008
Information verified and updated for 2010

Colour separation by Keenes, Andover, UK
Printed and bound by Leo Paper Products, China

A CIP catalogue record for this book is available from the British Library.

ISBN 978-0-7495-5490-3

Published by AA Publishing, a trading name of AA Media Limited, whose registered office is Fanum House, Basing View, Basingstoke, Hampshire RG21 4EA. Registered number 06112600.

A04019
Maps in this title produced from map data supplied by Global Mapping, Brackley, UK © Global Mapping
Transport map © Communicarta Ltd, UK

The Automobile Association wishes to thank the following photographers, companies and picture libraries for their assistance in the preparation of this book.

Abbreviations for the picture credits are as follows – (t) top; (b) bottom; (l) left; (r) right; (c) centre; (AA) AA World Travel Library.

Front cover Las Vegas News Bureau; **back cover (i)** Las Vegas News Bureau; **(ii)** AA/C Sawyer; **(iii)** AA/L Dunmire; **(iv)** AA/L Dunmire; **1** AA/C Sawyer; **2–18t** Las Vegas News Bureau; **4tl** Las Vegas News Bureau; **5b** Las Vegas News Bureau; **6cl** MGM Mirage; **6c** MGM Mirage; **6cr** Las VegasNews Bureau; **6bl** Las Vegas News Bureau; **6bc** MGM Mirage; **6br** Las Vegas News Bureau; **7cl** MGM Mirage; **7c** MGM Mirage; **7cr** AA/C Sawyer; **7bl** AA/L Dunmire; **7bc** AA/L Dunmire; **7br** Las Vegas News Bureau; **10ctr** AA/M Van Vark; **10cr** Las Vegas News Bureau; **10/11c** Las Vegas News Bureau; **10/11b** AA/L Dunmire; **11ctl** Las Vegas News Bureau; **11cl** AA/L Dunmire; **12b** Las Vegas News Bureau; **13(i)** Las Vegas News Bureau; **(ii)** Las Vegas News Bureau; **(iii)** Las Vegas News Bureau; **(iv)** Las Vegas News Bureau; **(v)** Las Vegas News Bureau; **14(i)** Las Vegas News Bureau; **(ii)** Las Vegas News Bureau; **(iii)** AA/L Dumire; **(iv)** Las Vegas News Bureau; **15b** Las Vegas News Bureau; **16(i)** AA/L Dunmire; **(ii)** AA/L Dunmire; **(iii)** Las Vegas News Bureau; **(iv)** Courtesy of The Venetian Resort-Hotel-Casino; **17(i)** AA/L Dunmire; **(ii)** MGM Mirage; **(iii)** MGM Mirage; **(iv)** Las Vegas News Bureau; **18ctr** Las Vegas News Bureau; **18cr** AA/L Dunmire; **18cbr** AA/L Dunmire; **18br** MGM Mirage; **19(i)** AA/L Dunmire; **(ii)** Las Vegas News Bureau; **(iii)** MGM Mirage; **(iv)** AA/L Dunmire; **(v)** AA/L Dunmire; **20/21** AA/L Dunmire; **24** MGM Mirage; **24/25** AA/M Van Vark; **25tr** MGM Mirage; **25c** Las Vegas News Bureau; **25cr** MGM Mirage; **26** MGM Mirage; **27t** Las Vegas News Bureau; **27cl** AA/L Dunmire; **27cr** MGM Mirage; **28t** Premier Exhibitions, Inc; **28cl** AA/C Sawyer; **28cr** Premier Exhibitions, Inc; **29t** AA/C Sawyer; **29cl** AA/C Sawyer; **29cr** Premier Exhibitions, Inc; **30l** Courtesy of the Liberace Foundation & Museum, Las Vegas; **30c** Las Vegas News Bureau; **30r** Courtesy of the Liberace Foundation & Museum, Las Vegas; **31l** Las Vegas News Bureau; **31r** Las Vegas News Bureau; **32tl** MGM Mirage; **32cl** MGM Mirage; **32/33t** MGM Mirage; **32/33c** MGM Mirage; **33tr** MGM Mirage; **33cr** MGM Mirage; **34–36t** Las Vegas News Bureau; **34bl** AA/L Dunmire; **34br** Las Vegas News Bureau; **35bl** Las Vegas News Bureau; **35br** MGM Mirage; **36bl** Las Vegas News Bureau; **36br** AA/L Dunmire; **37** AA/C Sawyer; **38t** AA/L Dunmire; **39–40t** AA/L Dunmire; **41–42t** AA/L Dunmire; **43** AA/C Sawyer; **46l** Las Vegas News Bureau; **46c** AA/L Dunmire; **46r** AA/L Dunmire; **47l** AA/L Dunmire; **47r** Las Vegas News Bureau; **48** MGM Mirage; **48/49t** MGM Mirage; **48/49c** MGM Mirage; **49tr** MGM Mirage; **49c** MGM Mirage; **49cr** AA/L Dunmire; **50l** Imperial Palace Auto Collections; **50r** Imperial Palace Auto Collections; **51l** AA/L Dunmire; **51c** AA/L Dunmire; **51r** Las Vegas News Bureau; **52** Las Vegas News Bureau; **53t** MGM Mirage; **53cl** MGM Mirage; **53cr** AA/L Dunmire; **54l** AA/L Dunmire; **54c** Las Vegas News Bureau; **54r** AA/L Dunmire; **55t** AA/C Sawyer; **55r** AA/C Sawyer; **56l** Courtesy of The Venetian Resort-Hotel-Casino; **56r** Courtesy of The Venetian Resort-Hotel-Casino; **56/57** AA/L Dunmire; **57t** Courtesy of The Venetian Resort-Hotel-Casino; **57c** Courtesy of The Venetian Resort-Hotel-Casino; **57cr** Courtesy of The Venetian Resort-Hotel-Casino; **58** AA/C Sawyer; **59–61t** Las Vegas News Bureau; **59b** Las Vegas News Bureau; **60bl** Las Vegas News Bureau; **60br** AA/C Sawyer; **61b** Las Vegas News Bureau; **62t** AA/L Dunmire; **63–64t** AA/L Dunmire; **64c** AA/L Dunmire; **65t** AA/L Dunmire; **66–68t** AA/L Dunmire; **69** Las Vegas News Bureau; **72l** AA/L Dunmire; **72tr** MGM Mirage; **72cr** MGM Mirage; **73t** MGM Mirage; **73cl** AA/L Dunmire; **73cr** AA/L Dunmire; **74l** Sahara Hotel & Casino; **74r** Sahara Hotel & Casino; **75l** AA/L Dunmire; **75r** AA/L Dunmire; **76l** Las Vegas News Bureau; **76r** Las Vegas News Bureau; **77l** AA/C Sawyer; **77c** AA/C Sawyer; **77r** AA/C Sawyer; **78** AA/L Dunmire; **79t** AA/C Sawyer; **79b** AA/C Sawyer; **80t** Las Vegas News Bureau; **81t** Las Vegas News Bureau; **82t** AA/M Van Vark; **83** AA/L Dunmire; **86tl** AA/L Dunmire; **86cl** AA/L Dunmire; **86cr** AA/L Dunmire; **86/87** AA/L Dunmire; **87cl** AA/L Dunmire; **87cr** AA/L Dunmire; **88l** Las Vegas News Bureau; **88r** AA/L Dunmire; **89l** Las Vegas Natural History Museum; **89r** Las Vegas Natural History Museum; **90t** AA/L Dunmire; **90b** Las Vegas News Bureau; **91t** AA/L Dunmire; **92t** Las Vegas News Bureau; **93t** Las Vegas News Bureau; **94/95** AA/M Van Vark; **98** Las Vegas News Bureau; **98/99t** US Department of the Interior, Bureau of Reclamation; **98/99c** AA/M Van Vark; **99** US Department of the Interior, Bureau of Reclamation; **100t** Las Vegas News Bureau; **100cl** AA/L Dunmire; **100c** AA/L Dunmire; **100cr** AA/L Dunmire; **101t** AA/L Dunmire; **101c** AA/L Dunmire; **102t** Mars Retail Group; **102bl** Mars Retail Group; **102br** AA/K Paterson; **103** AA/M Van Vark; **104t** AA/M Van Vark; **104b** AA/M Van Vark; **105t** AA/L Dunmire; **105b** AA/M Van Vark; **106t** Las Vegas News Bureau; **106c** Las Vegas News Bureau; **107** AA/L Dunmire; **108–112t** AA/C Sawyer; **108(i)** AA/L Dunmire; **(ii)** AA/L Dunmire; **(iii)** AA/L Dunmire; **(iv)** AA/L Dunmire; **113** Las Vegas News Bureau; **114–125t** Las Vegas News Bureau; **121bl** MRI Bankers' Guide to Foreign Currency, Houston, USA; **124bl** Las Vegas News Bureau; **124/125b** Hulton Archive/Getty Images; **125bc** Vernon Merritt III/Time Life Pictures/Getty Images; **125br** Jon Brennels/Time Life Pictures/Getty Images

Every effort has been made to trace the copyright holders, and we apologise in advance for any accidental errors. We would be pleased to apply any corrections in any following edition of this publication.